GET WHAT YOU WANT

Patricia Fripp

HDL PUBLISHING COMPANY

A Division of HDL COMMUNICATIONS,
Costa Mesa, CA 92626.

Printed in the United States of America.

ISBN 0-937359-54-8

DEDICATION

To my parents, Arthur and Edie Fripp, my cronies, Toyah, and my brother, Robert, who thinks this second edition should be called..."Take Quite A Bit More Charge Of Some Of Most Of A Lot Of The Rest Of Rather A Great Deal Of The Remaining Parts Of What's Left Of Your Life; Part Two."

ACKNOWLEDGMENTS

To Joel Margulis, to Becky Gordon, and to Joan Minninger and Eleanor Dugan for their invaluable editorial assistance.

FOREWORD

I hope you enjoy this book. It is all about possibilities. I hope the words inspire you to look at the possibilities in your own life.

CONTENTS

CHAPTER 1

If the World Were Perfect

> "*In terms of defining a personal aim, you should reflect on it, chew it over, and have it stretch your capacities—but make it within your reach.*"
>
> Robert Fripp

> "*There are no unrealistic goals; there are only unrealistic time frames.*"
>
> Don Hutson

Texas multi-millionaire H. L. Hunt was interviewed on a North Carolina television talk show some years back. Host Ty Boyd asked Hunt, "How have you amassed fortunes when most of us are struggling to make a living?" Hunt, who built the Houston Astrodome, replied, "You have to make up your mind what you want. You have to make up your mind what you are prepared to give up to get it. You have to set your priorities, and then go about your job."

That sounds too simple to be true. But think about it:

Decide what you want.

It amazes me that most people spend more time planning next summer's vacation than they do planning the rest of their lives. What do you want? What do you want to accomplish in your career, for yourself, or with your family? How do you want your life to be different in the future?

Defining "Success"

Nearly everyone wants to be *successful*, but few can define it. Does success involve money? On the basis of income, the average twelve-year-old drug dealer is then more successful than Ralph Nader, Mother Teresa, Shakespeare, or Martin Luther King, Jr. Does success mean power over other people's lives? Then a dedicated terrorist is just as successful as Gandhi, Lincoln, or the entire graduating class of a major medical school. Does success mean controlling how people think and act? Then pop stars (as John Lennon noted sadly in his often-misinterpreted remark) are certainly as successful as Jesus.

Obviously few people are eager to be *unsuccessful*, and just as obviously *success* needs some rigorous defining. You can start by understanding very specifically what you want. What *do* you want? Most people's responses are vague, almost generic. For instance:

I want more. More what? More than who? Exactly how much? Why? Then what?

I want things to be better. Better than what? Better how? What are your criteria? Better for whom?

I want to get ahead. Of whom? How? How will you know when you have gotten there? Then what?

I want so-and-so to be proud of me. A worthy goal and one that separates humans from amoebas, but are you sure that specific actions will produce the desired result? What specifically must you accomplish? How will you feel then? How will you feel when you reach your goal and so-and-so *isn't* proud of you? Does it make any difference?

I want people to respect me. The dictionary defines "respect" as "to revere, esteem, or admire." Which specifically do you want? For some people, having respect means that people notice, obey, or fear them. Do you want admiration or just attention? Esteem or, in reality, obedience? Do you want to be respected for a specific quality or a specific accomplishment? What are you going to do so that people will respond to you in this positive way? What if you carry out your plan and people don't react the way you want?

All of us must develop our own personal definition of success. Mine is this:

Success is feeling that if you had an unlimited amount of money, you would not change your friends, career, or lifestyle significantly.

Start with What You Don't Want

Knowing exactly what you want isn't always easy. When you are confused, you should start by making a list of what you know you *don't* want. Ask yourself whether you would be satisfied doing what you're doing now in five years. What if you are in the same kinds of relationships? What would be the logical progression in your job? What are your alternatives?

What Excites You?

Trish Britt, a well-known San Francisco public relations person, senses a fine line between succeeding and failing. She insists that it doesn't take much more of an effort to succeed than it does to fail. She showers people with questions they should be asking themselves: What do you like to do? What are your talents? What do you feel good about? What excites you? Then Britt warns, "Be realistic about where you can start. When you decide, really dedicate yourself to it and persist at it. No one is going to make you successful except yourself. If you're not trying, no one else will. If you're good at something and try very hard at it, you're going to succeed."

A wonderful man, Joe Heitz of Heitz Cellars, a well-known Napa Valley personality, urges us to pick something we like to do. "That's the first thing," he insists. "If you like winemaking, don't try to be a banker. If you like accounting, don't ride the rodeo circuit. Get into something you enjoy. It makes work—and life—so much more pleasant."

Choosing Goals

Asking yourself difficult questions is your first step in deciding what you want. The second step is formulating specific goals. Most people think of a goal as an end that can be reached once and for all. In fact, goals are more like road plans for progressing through life. Each goal takes you part of the way, keeps you on course, makes it harder to get lost.

Workable goals have two characteristics: They must be *challenging* and they must be *measurable*. Then, to be sure they are carried out, they need to be *concrete* (written down) and *shared* (co-authored).

Goals Should Be Challenging

You don't jump out of bed with enthusiasm on a Monday morning if your goal is simply to survive, to make enough money to pay your lousy bills. Survival can be challenging, but most people prefer to function at a higher level. On the other hand, the goal of quadrupling your salary next year may not be realistic.

This doesn't mean you will never do it, just that you might not do it *next* year. Goals should be challenging, but they also have to be attainable. So many people go to a seminar or they sit down with their sales managers or bosses to set goals, and they set them unrealistically high for the amount of energy they are prepared to put into them. Then, at year's end, they can say, "See, I told you it wouldn't work."

Goals Should Be Measurable

Be sure to keep track of your progress, so you know how you are doing. Have some sort of yardstick, not just subjective feelings that can be affected by mood swings or manipulated by outside criticism. If you are losing weight, making money, running — whatever it is — make sure you can measure your progress. Even people who dedicate their lives to enormous tasks — inventing the light bulb, curing cancer, promoting world peace — must break down their project into measurable units. Thomas Edison tested six thousand substances as potential filaments for the light bulb before he found one that worked. He viewed the rejects not as failures but as information that put him one step closer to what *would* work.

Goals Should Be Concrete

Your goals — all the things you want to accomplish — should be written down, so that every day you can affirm those goals. Writing things down also helps you to clarify your thinking and to define your goals more clearly. What is "more"? What is "better"? The simple act of writing the words and reading them back is the first concrete step toward achieving your goals.

Goals Should Be Shared

Finally, your goals in many cases should be co-authored with your family or co-workers. For example, there was no point in my setting a goal of having the most successful hairstyling shop in San Francisco if my staff did not want to work in one of the most successful salons. If you want to make changes in your organization or your department to be more efficient, get together with your colleagues and co-author your goals.

How to Get Hot

"I have seen people who remind me of the story about the wood-burning stove," says Cavett Robert, founder of the National Speakers Association. " They'll stand in front of the stove and say, 'Give me some heat and I'll give you some wood.' That's not the characteristic of a wood-burning stove. You have to put the wood in first. There is an observable difference between those who are successful and those who are unsuccessful. The unsuccessful are looking for pleasing experiences; the successful are looking for pleasing results. The unsuccessful do not want to study, do not want to take time away from pleasant things. Have a goal, know where you are going."

How to Make Life Better

A world-famous architect, Gyo Obata, once said to me, "The quality of life in the world could be improved, but too many people shoot for mediocre objectives. If everyone wanted a better environment, better places to live, better places to go to school, better places to work, I think we'd have a better world." I believe that all of us have much more power to improve and control our lives than we realize. Each one of us. Here are two examples of people who took charge of a situation and made it better.

Venita VanCaspel, first woman member of the Pacific Stock Exchange and author of *New Money Dynamics*: "The reason I find that people fail is failure to establish a goal. If you aim at nothing in life, you're just liable to hit it. I have never had anyone come up to me and say, 'Venita, I plan to fail,' but I've seen a lot of people fail to plan. And, unfortunately, you're going to end up the very same way. Always be prepared. I really do not believe in luck. Luck is when preparedness and opportunity get together."

When VanCaspel had completed her sales training, her manager handed her the phone book and told her to call people and sell to them. After one morning of cold calling, VanCaspel was getting neither pleasing results nor pleasing experiences. She decided there had to be a way better suited to her personality. She started giving seminars and talks in department stores, which turned out to be an incredible prospecting tool. It had never been done—nor has it been done since with as much success, though many people have copied VanCaspel's idea. She has spent years gathering wood for her stove.

Business consultant and international speaker Ted Anstedt, of Hillsborough, California, is somebody whose success I have watched grow and develop. He was only twenty-six in 1971 when I first met him. We were both sitting in the front row of a seminar. (I've always said that you meet the best people sitting in the front row at seminars.)

Ted Anstedt: "Determine what makes you tick, because this is what really helps you understand yourself and what your natural reactions are. The thing that drives me more than anything else is the desire for control over my own life and a certain lifestyle, rather than great wealth or power over other people.

"I see what happens in a lot of businesses. People go for a promotion here and a promotion there, moving all over the country, dragging their families around, and they end up combating frustrations, ulcers, and divorces. They're letting somebody else set their goals for them.

"Earl Nightingale came up with the best definition of success I ever heard and that was, 'the progressive realization of worthy ideals.' You need to break up those worthy ideals into separate areas and keep track of them. The times when I've been the most unhappy with myself and with my life have been when I lost track of the balance, when I began using money as a way of keeping score.

"Often in corporations, you begin to crave power. I see that a lot. I'm working with some of the world's biggest corporations—all the major computer companies, such as IBM and NCR. I see these tremendous power drives. I see the people who get caught in the game and lose sight of what their goals are. Or, they never had the goals in the first place. That's probably the key. I was least happy when I was unclear about my goals. You have to know yourself."

Ted Anstedt travels worldwide giving seminars and owns real estate with some of the most successful entrepreneurs in the real estate business. He and his friends used to get together on his birthday to drink and play Thumper, a popular drinking game, the sole purpose of which is to get thoroughly drunk. To celebrate his twenty-third birthday, he called his friends over, but for once they did not get drunk. Instead, they listened to an Earl Nightingale tape titled, "Think and Grow Rich." Then Ted asked his friends, "Now, what are we going to do with the rest of our lives? Let's start planning now."

I like to use this philosophy: "If life were perfect, what would it look like?" Not that it ever will, but we should look higher before we compromise.

Ten Minutes a Day

It's great to be young and have fun, but there is a time to grow up and get serious. Most people do not know what they want. That's where you start. Invest ten minutes a day thinking about:

☆ How can I make my job better?
☆ How can I know more about my job?
☆ How can I improve my career?
☆ How can I improve my marriage?
☆ How can I improve me?
☆ What do I have to learn?
☆ What do I want to eliminate?

The answers may not come in a flash, but it's important to get into the habit of asking the right questions. Just ten minutes a day, and you'll still have 1,430 minutes left.

Speed Traps

We all know life is not simple. No matter how well we plan or how hard we work, the unexpected is always lurking, ready to zap us. At times we get discouraged. That's why we need to surround ourselves with supportive people. But if you truly feel impatient about your progress over a long period, you should check for roadblocks.

1. *Check the Map.* If things aren't happening fast enough, take a moment to examine your goals. Are they realistic? Have you mapped out logical steps to achieve them? Naturally, good things don't come to those who just sit around and wait. You must create the energy that will get you what you want. Eventually, if your plans are logical, success will come to you.

2. *Check the Traffic.* If your plans seem logical and the goal reasonable, check to see that you're not being sidetracked by something else. Live, dream, and believe in your goals every single day. Don't spend too much time with low-priority items. Ask yourself, "What is the fastest, most efficient way to achieve my goal?" Then follow that road to the best of your ability.

3. *Check the Destination.* If you feel you are making too many sacrifices as your career progresses, perhaps you have focused on an inappropriate goal.

Choices, Not Sacrifices

In spite of the many years I have worked — and worked hard — I do not feel I have made too many sacrifices. I did make *choices*, however, based on what I knew was important to me. Many people have said, "Patricia, you are crazy to work as hard as you do." But for me, work — what I do — is my way of expressing myself.

No matter what you do, you must find some way in your life to express yourself at least part of the time. If you hate getting up in the morning, hate what you're doing, perhaps you should start looking for another job. But be sure that you have one area of your life in which you feel fulfilled — where you can express yourself.

When Are You a Success?

To an extent, I can think of myself as a success today because I have achieved many of my past goals. But there never is a final goal, and you never get "there" — the place where everything is accomplished and you no longer have to worry. That's the *fun* of it!

I'm often glad that I didn't know at the beginning what I know now, or I might never have started! But even though I've worked extremely hard and experienced ups and downs, most of the time I've been exceedingly happy.

Now then, let's get back to Mr. Hunt. Remember that Hunt said, "Make up your mind what you want."

What do you want? Set your priorities. Unless you know what you want, unless you know what your major goals are, unless you know the difference you can make in your future or your company's future, how on earth can you set priorities?

What is it worth? Make up your mind what you are prepared to give up to reach your goal. Even highly successful people can lack balance in their lives. If your family, your physical health, and your spiritual growth are as important to you as making money, you must allow time for these things. Scheduling becomes difficult when you don't know what is important to you.

When I have to make a decision, I ask myself how it will apply to my major goals. That is the test of whether I do it or not. For example, for several years I belonged to a dynamic women's organization in San Francisco. We had a fundraiser that lost money. (Not exactly the way to prove to the world that we were successful entrepreneurs.) I must hasten to add, I did not help plan this fundraiser, but I did have a few good suggestions about how to raise money to make up the deficit. As a result of that, a couple of women on the board said, "Patricia, you are so creative, we should have you for our president."

Well, for a moment, perhaps five minutes, I wallowed in the glory: "President Fripp" sounded oh so appropriate. After that, I thought, "But, how will it affect my two current major goals?"

Goal One: Would I be able to run my hairstyling salon more successfully if I spent the time necessary to be president of the organization?

Answer: Not really, because the organization would take at least eight hours a week of the time that I could be in my shop. Certainly the visibility in the organization would be good for business, but I was making myself visible anyway; it wouldn't make that much difference.

Goal Two: Would being president help promote my speaking career?

Answer: Not really. Even though it would be a good experience running meetings, I would have to turn down paid speaking engagements.

You can guess my decision. When you know what you want, it's easy to find out what your priorities are.

Success as a Process

Too many people think of success as a goal to be reached once and for all, rather than a process, a way of living. A very successful New York businesswoman, Eva Stern, once said, "Don't believe that you're going to open your own business and live happily ever after. That's what they used to tell us about marriage!"

Eva is a wise woman. She realizes that simply achieving your goal doesn't guarantee that you'll be happy — or successful. Both happiness and success are processes, ways of life. And for any entrepreneur, man or woman, the success and happiness come from a succession of achievements which have been carefully planned and logically worked out. If you are not content at every step of your ladder to success, you're not going to be happy when you get there. This is something I try never to forget.

At age fifteen, I prepared for my career by cutting our neighbors' hair, rather than concentrating entirely on dating and other standard teenage activities. (I don't want to sound like a martyr—I *did* date—but I didn't spend a lot of time and energy out looking for "fun.") I used to think, "Well, when I'm a good hairstylist, then I'll have more time to play." Then it became "when I finish my book . . . " or "when I've worked on this project or that project. . . . " Now, over two decades later, I realize that everything I do is fun, that I'm not postponing pleasure until I reach a goal. This is important because people *never* reach their goals! Before you get "there," you reset your goals so you can stretch and grow beyond them.

Norman Lear, the highly successful American television producer, says, "Success is how you collect your minutes. You spend millions of minutes to reach triumph. Then you spend a thousand minutes enjoying it. If you were unhappy through those millions of minutes, what good are the thousands of minutes of triumph? Happiness is made of tiny successes, like good eye contact with your wife over breakfast. The big ones come too infrequently. If you don't have zillions of tiny successes, the big ones don't mean a thing."

Feelings of success come from the satisfaction of constant growth toward a goal that you set for yourself. The older I get, the more I recognize the possibility of accomplishing practically anything in my own realm. Naturally, I can't expect to become a brain surgeon. At my age, with my lack of education, the hurdles would be too great. I also would love to sing like Barbra Streisand, but even in the shower I sound more like R2-D2. However, I do have the necessary skills, energy, and ambition to be a dynamic public speaker. When you set your goals within your own abilities, you *can* achieve them—if you are committed.

When I left school, one goal I had was never again to do anything even slightly athletic because I hated field hockey and all the other games we had had to play. Anything athletic was against my nature. But many of my friends had talked about the value of running. Although I enjoyed running, I had never run more than a mile at any one time.

Somehow—and I don't know quite where it came from—I realized I wanted to be a runner to prove to myself I could do anything I set my mind to do. I wanted to run. I wanted its benefits. I realized I didn't have to be a marathon runner to be healthy, but I wanted to prove to myself that I could do what I really (and realistically) desired. I wanted to do something that was unnatural for me. Now, I am completely addicted, have achieved half-marathons, and feel it's the best way to start the day.

Remember H. L. Hunt's rule: *Make up your mind what you want.* To do this, you have to look to the future and see what you want. Change is inevitable. With the changes that are coming in your company, in the country, in your family, in yourself, how do you want your life to be? Your goals should be challenging, attainable, measurable, co-authored (in writing), and positive.

Interested . . . or Committed?

Ken Blanchard, author of *The One Minute Manager*, addressing the National Speakers Association in San Francisco, asked, "Do you have an interest in what you say you want? Or is it a commitment? If you have an *interest in*, you do what you have to when you feel like it or when it's convenient. With a *commitment to*, you don't have to ask, 'Do I feel like following through today?'"

A Goal or a Fantasy?

Three of my pals and I — we met at a seminar years ago — used to get together for lunch every few months to formalize our goals and check each other's progress. For his health goal, one of the cronies kept saying that he wanted to trek through the Himalayas. I would reply, "I won't let you write that down as a goal — you don't even go backpacking!"

Danny Cox, a top speaker, says we have to know the difference between a goal and a fantasy: "With a *goal* you do what you can do tomorrow to get you closer to it. A *fantasy* is something you sit in a bubblebath with and dream about." Both have places in our lives. Let's just not confuse one with the other.

YOUR ASSIGNMENT:
Think About What You Want

Goals in life for _____

Date: _____

Financial Goals:

First step:
Timetable:

Physical Goals:

First step:
Timetable:

Career Goals:

First step:
Timetable:

Family and Social Goals:

First step:
Timetable:

Personal Growth Goals:

First step:
Timetable:

☆ Things I am willing to sacrifice to achieve my goals:

☆ Things I am NOT willing to sacrifice to achieve my goals:

☆ People I would like to get involved in my goals:

☆ Ways I will reward myself as I come closer to reaching my goals:

CHAPTER 2

Taking Responsibility for Yourself

> *"Clearly define the long-range goals you
> aspire to, and all the obstacles in your way
> will become hills instead of mountains."*
>
> O. A. Battista

Many people like to blame their problems on others. Parents usually rank first as scapegoats, followed in later years by hostile employers and rejecting lovers. Now, most parents do the best they can, raising their children the way they were brought up themselves. The mistakes they make result more from lack of knowledge than actual malice. Employers and lovers also have their own agendas and needs that don't always coincide with our own.

As adults, we are responsible for our own choices, feelings, and self-esteem. Like it or not, we are the only ones in charge of our actions. It may be very comforting to see others as the manipulators of our behavior and the source of all our woes, but it is a real timewaster. The day that you discover that *you* are in charge of you is the day you turn your life around.

What Kind of World Do You Live In?

The type of person you are is the type of world you live in. Your perception of the world *is* your world. To turn a popular expression around, "What you get is what you see."

How you interpret and react to problems is a strong clue to your personality. John Coe, president of Integrated Target Marketing in

Chicago, divides the various approaches to problems into what he calls the "dented fender philosophy." If there's a dent in the fender, you have several choices.

Responses to Dented Fender

1. Try to find out who did it.

2. Call the insurance company.

3. Fix it.

4. Leave it and keep going.

Of course, knowing where and why the fender got dented may help you avoid future dents, but Coe's view is that it doesn't matter *how* the fender got dented. It *is* dented. Now that it's done, what are you going to do about it? It's a nuisance — it's worse than a nuisance — but why spend energy being angry and upset when it's more productive to accept the problem and either fix it or go on?

Coe says, "If I find out that a salesperson has been taking the company for a ride, doesn't have much paperwork to do, or doesn't make many sales, I can sit down with him or her and begin by slapping wrists. But, that's like the dented fender. The first thing for us to do is consider what we can do *now* to bring him or her up to an acceptable level. What's over with can't be changed. Learn from those things and do it better in the future.

"You know, my father had two opportunities in his life. One was to be a professional golfer. When he was eighteen, he beat the world-famous champion, Bobby Jones, but he decided against a golf career. The other opportunity was a chance to join the Office of Strategic Services — the famed OSS — during the war. He turned both down. From then on, he was convinced he was a failure. And he was — *because* he concentrated on those two events for the rest of his life. He wasted his life walking backward into the future. Today is the only thing you can do something about."

I share Coe's sentiments. I get impatient with people who hang onto the same problems. If they spent as much energy being productive as they spend hanging onto their problems, they would be successful.

For some people, being unsuccessful or ordinary is easier because they know how that feels. It's comfortable. They maintain negative ideas about what successful people are like: hard — cold — calculating. Or, knowing how many workers feel about supervisors, they console themselves with: "I would rather go along with the crowd than manage people who will criticize me." But Werner Erhard says, "You will go crazy if you worry about what everybody else says about you." Erhard has also pointed out that "people either have the results that they want in life or all the reasons for not having them."

Choices—Even in Prison

Former San Quentin inmate Robert Perry Frogge provides a perfect example of Erhard's principle. In 1976 Frogge was in San Quentin Prison. He had been there for eleven years: "I had 'life' with no possibility of parole. I took a program called *est*, and during the training I got in contact with the fact that I was in San Quentin because that's where I should be. I started looking at my life and said, 'Okay, I'm here for kidnap, robbery, without possibility of parole. I've got an Indiana hold, a Federal hold, a Marin County hold. I'm fixed for life. I know what it takes to stay here in San Quentin. So if I'm creating my life and I want to get out of prison, what is it going to take?' I came to the conclusion that I had to do just the opposite of what I'd been doing. Instead of trying to escape (I had tried many times), fighting with the cops, being a pain in the neck, I had to say, 'I've got to start doing something positive.'

"So I got involved with the youth program in 1976, started going to college, and got my degree in prison. In other words, I started giving something back. I just started being concerned about others, especially convicts and street people. I started giving of myself—in letters, telephone calls, visits. In August of 1976, they changed the law; suddenly I had the possibility of parole. In two and one-half years, I was out of San Quentin.

"Once I started creating miracles in my life, things started falling into place. I got involved with a lot of public service programs. I took transcendental meditation, Dale Carnegie, and psychodrama. I became aware that many kids are into drugs, so I took a drug abuse program and by the second year I was a counselor. I counseled other convicts and I started giving what I wanted out of life. I've been getting it back ever since.

"I came out of prison on December 22, 1980. I got married on December 31, 1980, and I was released from the halfway house March 9, 1981. I probably have more today and am happier than I have ever been in my life. And I know everything I've got I deserve. I want to make positive use of what knowledge and experience I have had.

"One thing I've learned is that people really play games with themselves. You can talk to 95 percent of the guys in prison and they'll tell you it's either their mommy's fault, their daddy's fault, their race, or their environment—they'll have a million excuses why they got screwed up. Very few of them will really come out and tell you that they're responsible and they are there because they want to be there. Some will say they are responsible but didn't haul themselves off to prison. They don't see the connection.

"You know, it's easy to be responsible when you're happy and have things like you want them. But being responsible when you're really in trouble, that's something else. It's a funny thing: Even millionaires will tell you how bad things are — taxes, inflation, IRS, the Republicans, whatever. *Nothing is ever anyone's own fault.*

"But I believe your actions determine what's going to happen to you in your life. An inmate, a close friend of mine, George, had been in prison fourteen years. He had thirty days to go when he was provoked, got into a fight, and beat up another inmate. When George went to sleep later that night, this guy crept up on him, stabbed him in the eye, and killed him. How stupid — just a little two-bit fist fight. How easy it is to get killed in there. I was living in an open dorm and I thought in one second I could lose it. In one second of madness, George lost it: He had played that other guy's game, then got into the fight and lost his life.

"I have been close myself. There were just too many times that I should have gotten killed. In one escape attempt, I remember, we were being transported, and we jumped the driver and the other marshal. The driver hit the brakes and somehow kept the car on the road. There were five of us in the car. I don't know to this day what kept us from getting killed.

"I finally came to realize that if I smile at people and am happy with people and treat people right, I've got 99 chances out of 100 that they'll be the same way, because you get back what you put out. At times, I think what I'm doing now doesn't make a difference. The world is going to go on or it's going to explode. But I think you can make a difference in your own life and how you feel about yourself. If I can leave this old world a better place, then it's worthwhile.

"I gained more from the agony of prison than I ever have gained from anything else in my life. I am a professor when it comes to prison and the games that people play on themselves. The first eleven years that I was in prison, I served every second. The last five years, it served me every second."

Frogge was with me when I returned to San Quentin in July 1986 to talk to the inmates ready to be paroled. He was still trying to help other people. Recently I visited his home. He has a beautiful baby boy and a good career in the Bay Area selling cars at Melrose Ford in Oakland. Groups often hire him to share his philosophy with them.

"Shame on You"

A woman I know was mistreated by her alcoholic parents. When she was seven, her parents placed her in a foster home, where she was literally treated like a servant. She had to work from the moment she got up in the morning until she went to school. She had to work from the time she returned from school until she went to bed. There was very little joy in her childhood.

At age seventeen she cleaned a beauty school to pay her tuition there. When she graduated, she proved to be very talented and attracted many customers to her new employer's beauty shop. However, she was shy and didn't talk much about herself with her clients. One day a very special woman sat in her chair — a woman who was able to draw out her story and who was sincerely interested in her well-being. After she told this woman about her life, the client looked intently at her and said, "Shame on your parents for doing what they did to you! And shame on *you* if you let that affect your life any longer!"

Admittedly, some of us have a much better start in life than others, but nobody ever told us life was going to be fair. Life is the way it is. It is never too late to make a positive start: think about what you want to accomplish, set a plan, and take action.

Who Has the Solution?

Phil Steffen, a speaker from Atlanta, insists that there is one person who can solve 93 percent of your problems: *you*. We could solve the vast majority of our problems, he believes, if we were not so adept at manufacturing excuses: "People can rationalize anything."

Steffen tells the story of two Irishmen painting a building across the road from a house of ill repute. They see a Protestant minister enter the house, and they say, "Tut, tut, tut. How terrible." Then they see a rabbi go in and they say, "He's not a Christian, but still, he's a man of God. Tut, tut. What next?" Then they see a Catholic priest go in and they say, "I wonder who died?"

Our perceptions of the world become our world. They can brighten the dark corners or cast impenetrable gloom over the most luminous parts. The message is clear, isn't it? No matter what you do, *be responsible for yourself.*

Dr. Leonard Zunin, author of *Contact: The First Four Minutes*, says, "The more one perceives his or her behavior and fate as dominated by friends, business associates, wife, husband, children, mother-in-law, mysterious vibrations from outer space, or circumstances beyond one's control, the greater the chance for disappointment and misfortune."

Stop making excuses! Stand on your own two feet. Believe you can do it. As Winston Churchill said, "Never, never, never, never, never give up!" There are going to be many setbacks in your progress toward your business and personal goals. You're going to make mistakes. But that's how you learn. That's how you grow.

Afraid of a Challenge

Shirley Davalos made an opportunity for herself and then panicked and said, No. It took her five hard years before she made another opportunity.

When Shirley got out of college, she wanted to get into television. Everyone told her to start in a small town, but she went straight to San Francisco. There she got an interview at a local radio station and was offered a job — as a producer!

Shirley gulped. "What would the job entail?"

She was told that she would be responsible for calling important people like the mayor and asking them to appear on the show. "For instance, if the mayor is involved in a breaking news story, you'll call her up and ask her to be on the show the next day."

"I couldn't do that," Shirley said. "I've never done it before. I don't know how. Couldn't I start with something lower?" Her potential employer showed her the door. It was five years before she got another job offer in television.

During those five years she worked in several banks, still going for interviews at radio and television stations. Finally she got a job as receptionist at KBHK-TV, a local station. Once in the door, she went to every department offering her services. "I'm just sitting here most of the time," she'd say. "Is there anything I can do to help you?" She became a production assistant, making the same kind of phone calls that had panicked her five years earlier. She also started writing the movie vignettes for the newspapers.

Now that she knew people in the business, she learned about a production secretary job at KGO-TV, an ABC affiliate. It was only for three months, replacing a woman on maternity leave, but Shirley decided to risk it. She survived the three months and stayed with KGO-TV, eventually becoming a production secretary on the morning program, *A M San Francisco*. As the program grew in importance, Shirley did too, becoming its producer three years later.

"We had terrific management that let us work out ideas on the program. They guided us, instead of constantly telling us what was wrong. Our production team was incredible. We were really an us-against-the-world team and we worked hard. When a news story broke on the front page of the newspaper, you knew it would be on *A M San Francisco* that morning too. We 'made news.' When Pope John Paul II was shot, we had a ham radio operator getting us information directly from the Vatican. No one else in the nation had anything like that. But then the station management changed. The new people wanted us to do more fluff, more homemaker stuff."

Shirley wasn't always successful in putting her team together. "In one department I took over, the staff was in disarray. I couldn't pull them together into a team because management played favorites with many of them, turning them into backstabbers. No one would turn to help anyone else or warn them about something coming up. Everyone played for himself. The key to teamwork is that you are all working toward the same end."

Eventually Shirley decided to take another big step and start her own company, Orion Express. The Sausalito firm acts as consultant to people who want to present themselves on radio, television, or on national publicity tours. For instance, book publishers send her authors who have written fabulous books but who need help doing successful television interviews.

Using her background as a television producer, Shirley gets these people ready to go out and perform, to sell their books, and to take control of interviews. Her clients learn how to get their points across, even if the interviewer hasn't read the book. Her firm also produces "video resumes" for actors, public speakers, and public figures who appear frequently on television. Orion Express makes up composite tapes to show the range of the person's work. For example, an actor might offer some of the best scenes he has been in, or a public speaker might include portions of speeches. For someone who wants to promote an organization, product, or service on television with guest appearances, Orion will string together "air checks" to show producers the versatility, style, and exuberance of the potential guest.

Orion also produces video news releases. Right now a lot of television stations are cutting back on "soft news" for budget reasons. Soft news are the human interest stories about celebrity appearances, promotional events, ugly dog contests, and the like. Shirley's firm puts together modern versions of the traditional press release and sends them out by satellite to stations around the country that lack the staff to produce their own features.

So Shirley Davalos has brought herself a long way from the shy young woman who didn't think she would have the nerve to telephone the mayor. She has two pieces of advice for others:

1. *Don't be in love with a title*. Be in love with your work. Many people go into television and think it's going to be a glamorous job, that it's going to do this or that for them, but they're looking for ego, not work.

2. *Persevere*. That's how I got into television. My father said, "The last key on the ring that opens the door is perseverance. You can have luck, you can have success, you can have lots of different things, but if you continue to work at it, something is going to work out."

Shirley Davalos could have sat around the rest of her life, recalling how luck had been against her or how she had blown her one lucky break, but she made herself responsible for her own life. She followed her own two mottos: she persevered and she ignored the job title to get herself inside the door that she wanted.

YOUR ASSIGNMENT:
Dented Fender Incidents in My Life

"The most painful process known to man is thought."

Dr. Norman Vincent Peale

1. What dented fender incidents am I still concentrating on?

From high school:

From upsetting romances:

From my relationship with my family:

From my first job:

From my education — or lack of it:

From my relationship with my mate:

Other:

2. What single action will most help me grow at this time in my life?

3. What is the first thing I am going to let go of?

4. What is my first step?

5. Who is the first person I am going to forgive?

6. How will I reward myself when I do some of these things?

CHAPTER 3

Coping With and Creating Change

"Oh, God, why don't I remember that a little chaos is good for the soul?"

Marilyn French,
The Women's Room

"One of the changes of today is that women are becoming the men they used to want to marry."

Gloria Steinem

No one is a stranger to change. It visits us daily. Its challenge is so consuming of our daily lives that few have the luxury of contemplating its size or speed.

A skillful study of the enormous impact of change on this society can be found in *The Inner American, A Self-Portrait from 1957 to 1976*, by Joseph Veroff, Elizabeth Douvan, and Richard A. Kulka. The authors see less optimism in the future, less willingness to postpone happiness, less belief in doing what seems best for the society as a whole. These new attitudes have woven themselves into the fabric of American society, bringing profound changes in every aspect of our lives. The disintegration of our whole society is hardly imminent, but a sense of decline is naggingly persistent.

In *New Rules in American Life: Searching for Self-Fulfillment in a World Turned Upside-Down*, Daniel Yankelovich says that "there has been a significant shift in Americans' attitudes toward work and success in a relatively short period of time." The number of people who are sure that hard work always pays off is declining. Our basic belief in the "giving/getting tradeoff" is undergoing a marked change. With far fewer "traditional" families (male-dominated, one breadwinner), with the majority of women now working outside the home, with more women attending universities and graduate schools, the "continuity of the American experience" has been broken "in decisive ways."

These changes are not necessarily good or bad. They are simply changes. My point is to draw your attention to them, and my concern is with how you react to change. Ignoring change, pretending that nothing is going on, won't prevent it. Change is constant, one of the few things in life we can count on.

We are now nearing the 1990s. We have seen a lot of changes in the last half-century, but far fewer than the changes caused by the French and American revolutions, the industrial revolution, the abolition of slavery and child labor, the establishment of general literacy, women's suffrage, electric lighting, automobiles, airplanes, indoor plumbing, and the discovery of antibiotics, but changes nonetheless in a world that we have become familiar with. There is a change in the government. There is a change in economics. There is a change in the business climate, a change in morals, a change in ethics, a change in women's roles (and therefore a change in men's). We look around and wonder what to do with all this change.

Three Ways to Think About Change

1. Know that change of some kind is inevitable, and that it is often good and healthy.

2. Participate in change. Be eager to make a difference in your personal life, your company, your organization, your country. Don't react from necessity, letting events and other people dictate your life. React by thinking, planning, and taking action.

3. Believe strongly that you can make a difference.

The Excitement of Change

In 1977, Mary Healy was an unhappy teacher. Then she founded Women on the Run, Inc., a company offering everything from women's running apparel to women's running and fitness programs.

Healy thinks that people sometimes get a "stuck mentality." "They don't seek change," she says, "and as a result they are not exciting people to be around. The key to success is risk taking. If you measure rewards in something other than money, then you have a whole world to win.

"If you sit around and prop your feet up on a desk, you won't accomplish anything. Certainly the sense of urgency that entrepreneurs experience can quickly evolve into a sense of panic. My father had his own business for eighteen years. He had crisis points along the way, but he retained an underlying sense of optimism. I learned a great deal from his attitude. Sometimes it takes a good night's sleep or a decent movie or a nice long walk to put things into focus, to put you back on track, ready to face whatever problems arise, knowing that you can handle them."

Facing change and the problems created by change makes having an ultimate goal indispensable. You must at least have a picture of what you want your life to be like (if the world were perfect). On those days when you ask yourself, What the hell am I doing this for? Why am I suffering this way? you will have an answer because you have a goal.

So what are you waiting for?

Taking Risks

In *Risking*, David Viscott says, "If your life is ever going to be better, you have to take risks. There is simply no way you can grow without doing so. It is surprising how little most people know about taking risks. Often people become inhibited by the fear that, any moment, they must commit themselves to action. At the first sign of reversal, they damn themselves, hesitate, feeling that the situation is about to fall apart, retreat untested and protest they were in over their heads, thankful just to escape. They do not understand that to risk is to exceed one's usual limits. The uncertainty and danger are simply a part of the process."

Viscott adds, "We hold onto bad habits because we are not really committed to growing. We need an excuse for our failures. We keep our bad habits because we do not really love ourselves."

People find it difficult to abandon any investment—in money, love, time, effort, or commitment. But, we outgrow many things, and when that happens we don't have to consider these investments a waste. They were the things that made us who we are today. As Max Gunther relates in *The Luck Factor*, "A Swiss banker, a self-made millionaire, summed up his investment philosophy thus: If you are losing a tug of war with the tiger, give him the rope before he gets your arm. You can always buy a new rope."

The Fascination of Change

I find that the most fascinating people are those who create changes. Photographer Jack Peterson's life changed incredibly because he reached beyond the average. He started working for the telephone company over twenty years ago as a lineman. Unfortunately, he kept falling off the poles. "I just couldn't seem to stay up," he explains. "They figured they'd better get rid of me before I got hurt, so I became a splicer's helper (an assistant to the person in the manholes who puts wires together). I worked as a splicer for ten years or so and after that I went into management. But what I loved was photography.

"The phone company wanted me to stop taking time off for my photography — I said I couldn't do it. Finally, we came to an agreement. We had everything all worked out. Then disaster: I found out I had cataracts. Within eight months, I had operations on both eyes. It took me about a year to get back on my feet. That gave me time to think. Everything looked closed off. I decided to take a big risk. I went out on my own and filmed a historical documentary for the phone company. I spent about three or four weeks working on it. I filmed it, produced it, knocked at all the doors, and finally had it produced through the phone company. I got to the right people and said, 'Look, this is something you're going to want many years from now.' At last they said, 'Okay.'

"That opened the door for producing more films, and now I'm so busy I can barely keep up, especially with lecturing and starting a system called video chrome viewing. I found a way to eliminate the expense of bad pictures, and by putting our transparencies to music, we have what amounts to videotaped weddings. People love it!"

From telephone lineman to manager to successful photographer to lecturer. And what does he tell his fellow craftsmen? "You have to study your craft, whatever it may be. I started studying with an internationally famous photographer on the East Coast, Monty. I wanted to learn his techniques so I attended a lot of his seminars. Once he said, 'You here again? You must be slow.' 'No, I'm not,' I replied. 'I just believe in what you do.'"

Being in Control

Right about now some of you may be devising mental lists of all the events and tragedies that we *don't* have control over. How can you control the actions of others? Of fate? What if a building fell on you or your plane crashed or a stranger decided to shoot you?

Sharon Komlos can tell you that, short of death, you still have control over your life in the midst of tragedy. Sharon was shot and blinded by a total stranger who left her for dead.

Until what she calls her "incident," Sharon had lived a fairly routine life. In 1980 she had just turned thirty years old. She had been married ten years and had three children. One evening she was driving home at forty-five miles per hour down a road in Florida. A car pulled up next to her and she noticed a flash of light: "I felt the warm sensation of blood dripping down my face and I couldn't see. I pulled the car over to the side of the road and laid on the horn to summon help.

"Instantly a man appeared, lifted me off the car horn, and said he would take me to the hospital. He helped me out of my car and put me on the back seat floor of his car. I didn't know at the time that this was the guy who had shot me. He offered to help me as a good Samaritan.

I thought he was taking me to the hospital, as we drove around. I knew the area and I tried to direct him, although I couldn't see. When he stopped, he lifted me out of the car and helped me up some stairs, through a door. I realized later it was his apartment. He closed the door, and pushed me down on the mattress.

"I had no purse with me, nothing. We struggled. He tried to suffocate me first, but when I managed to break loose, he stabbed me in the chest, sliced me around the neck, and raped me. He kept me in his apartment for eight hours. When morning came, he left me for dead because I had lost so much blood. In the morning he checked my pulse and must have been satisfied with what he had found.

"He left me for dead in his apartment. The police said he probably had left to find a way to dispose of my body. He took my clothes. I got up and walked around the apartment and found my way out onto a balcony. I started screaming.

"Another man came and took me to the hospital. The police made out a search warrant for the apartment based on my description of what I had heard and felt. I hadn't been able to see anything since the flash on the road."

Before this traumatic event, Sharon Komlos was an insurance adjuster. "I used to go to body shops and estimate damage. I really had a man's job. I dealt with attorneys and I loved it. I did all my own investigations, all my own negotiations.

"So when I couldn't see any more, my employer thought I was no longer of any use. I was automatically let go and my desk was cleaned out before I even left the hospital. I was not even given the opportunity to prove what I was still capable of doing.

"I met Wayne Dyer, the author of *Your Erroneous Zones*, about one year later. We were introduced through a mutual friend. He told me I had much to offer and should consider sharing my strength with others. Through speaking he introduced me in Detroit and Cleveland on stage and the response was phenomenal."

Sharon became a speaker and wrote a book, *Feel the Laughter* (Trillium Press). But even that wasn't simple. She had many obstacles to overcome, including the breakup of her marriage. I asked her whether she is a different person now. "I'm not any different. It hasn't changed my outlook. But my husband had a difficult time dealing with me. We tried to work with it, but he couldn't handle it and I don't fault him in any way.

"In the hospital, the doctor told me, 'Sharon, you're going to be blind for the rest of your life.' I said, 'Well, yes I have already come to terms with that fact.' The doctor told me that the retinas were both completely destroyed.

"My brother saw the impact this had on my parents. They too were victims of this crime. All of us would have to learn how to deal with its aftermath. My family would have to learn from my example.

"My kids were nine, eight, and three. The hardest thing was trying to relate to my youngest child. One day her mother is driving her around doing everything and the next day she can't even see.

"When I started speaking, a lot of women who have been through a crisis inquired how I have managed. I say, 'I just do it.' But I have formulated ways for people to overcome problems in their lives by what works for me.

"These are my three basic philosophies. First, I accept what was handed down to me. I look at it as a challenge, as something that was given to me to learn about life.

"The second philosophy is that I cannot control the external forces around me, but I do control the path that my life is going to take. I have options. I am in control.

"The third is that everything happens for a reason. The reasons may not be apparent at the moment the incident occurs, but they will surface eventually. Everything does have a purpose.

"Since the attack, my philosophy has made me believe in myself more and, in some respects, has strengthened me. As time has passed, I have learned to trust my inner instincts more. I've always been my own person. I now fall into that category that is 'disabled' because I am blind. But I don't permit sympathy from my friends. I have found that the only limitations placed on me are in the minds of others. I have become an expert at overcoming. I had to build an entirely new career for myself, and the odds were not in my favor.

"People ask me how I cope with life. I say, 'I don't cope. I don't like just coping. I achieve.' I don't like the word 'coping.' It implies you're just going along at an even pace. I like the words 'succeeding' and 'achieving.' I want to do something beyond coping.

"After I was shot, I could have turned to drugs, alcohol, or suicide, but to me, life is precious. It's important for me to be here for my children and to experience what life has to offer. If there's a setback, the next moment it becomes part of your past which you can't change. And it's up to you how much you want your past to interfere with your present."

Creating Your Own Change

I have always had a great faith in life — that things work out the way they are supposed to. I believe we have choices. I believe we set goals and design our lives, that we create change as well as react to it. I believe that there is a certain order to the universe; I believe that there are few accidents.

Some things have been difficult, and I have had a few traumas in my life, but I've always had the feeling that there was a reason for most lessons in my life. The people in my life mean something to me. I hope and trust that I am playing an important part in their lives as they are playing a part in mine. I would not for a moment suggest that anyone believe everything I believe. I do encourage people to think and read and research alternatives so that they can make up their minds for themselves. You can't change the world but you can change yourself, and if you change yourself, suddenly you find the world has changed.

YOUR ASSIGNMENT:
Coping With and Creating Change

"It is not because things are difficult that we do not dare. It is because we do not dare that they are difficult."

Seneca

1. What has been the most difficult change for me to accept?

2. What fears about this change were unfounded?

3. What good things have come out of this change?

4. What has been the best change in my life?

5. Why was it the best?

6. What did I learn?

7. How did people around me respond to this change?

8. What positive things did I learn from this change?

9. How do I plan to accept change in the future?

10. What is the dumbest thing I ever did that I have learned something from?

11. Do I believe that change is good and necessary?

12. What will I do tomorrow to begin feeling more comfortable with change?

13. Do I plan to be one of the people in my industry who helps to control change?

14. Am I confident that I can handle any change I might face in the future?

CHAPTER 4

Cracking Your Comfort Barrier

> *"Those changes which may cause us the most immediate discomfort, often do us the most good in the long run."*
>
> O. A. Battista

You have to go past your "comfort zone," as Jim Newman of PACE Seminars calls it, if you are going to adapt to change. Change makes us uncomfortable. That's why we so often return to old, unproductive habits, rather than find something new.

Adapting to change is going to make you feel uneasy, distressed, even miserable. This discomfort is absolutely necessary before you can become the person you want to be. If you are going to make a difference in your company or your country, you are signing on for some discomfort.

It's okay to feel uncomfortable. If you think back on the most successful times in your life and how you felt before that success, you'll realize you were darned uncomfortable. That's because you were walking on new ground.

The Key to Adapting

Knowing what you want is the key to adapting successfully to new situations. When you know where you are going, you can handle the rough spots as you adapt and set up your future. Some of the best decisions I've made in my life — leaving England to come to America, opening a business, investing in real estate, becoming a public speaker — were terrifying at the time, but having a goal made the changes much less difficult.

When I was waving good-bye to my mother, I had no idea when we would see each other again. I told her not to cry because I knew if she did, I would. My father kept asking, "How do you know it will be better? What if you don't get a job? You won't be able to call your mother every day." Things were nice for me in England. I enjoyed home. I had a good job. I was comfortable. I had a nice boyfriend and lots of friends. But something in me insisted I go exploring. I was uncomfortable leaving, but I knew that it was what I had to do.

Handling the Discomfort

Achieving success is not a painless process, but it's usually worth it. (Ask a woman three months after she has had a baby whether it hurt. She can't remember. Nature has a way of blocking out pain with the thrill of the child; otherwise, few women would brave a second pregnancy.) To follow through on my resolves for change I had to get out of my "comfort zone." We all do.

In a time management seminar, I once asked the participants why they were there. One woman said, "Well, I am successful, but I'm comfortable. I want to learn how to get *un*comfortable so I can be even more successful."

The Cinderella Complex by Colette Dowling poses a critical question: "How, when we have dared nothing in life, do we begin to dare? What gives us the little push, the impetus to move out to the edge of what's familiar and then step beyond?" When I came to the United States I was twenty, didn't have a job, didn't know anyone, didn't have anywhere to live, and had $500. But I knew that everyone in America was rich. I was a little figure on a big boat going to America for a new life. It was the best decision I ever made.

Stretching Yourself

In 1975 I started demonstrating haircuts. At my first public demonstration, three snips into the haircut, I cut a big hole in my finger. Blood was oozing, but I finished the haircut. I had to keep stopping to mop my finger with a towel. Fortunately, my model had black hair! At other times I have cut hair in front of people who were totally unimpressed. I didn't like those feelings of failure and rejection and embarrassment. But I got up again and again and again until I made it worthwhile for those watching—and worthwhile for myself.

Even now, I frequently get nervous five minutes before a speaking engagement. It doesn't matter how many times I have done it before or will do it again. Five minutes before I go on, I look out at the people (sometimes they are corporate presidents and make four times as much money as I do), and I think nervously, I was invited to tell them how to run their businesses more successfully!

Do you know why I do it? One of the reasons is that the person who sits down after giving the talk is not the person who stood up to deliver the talk, and the person who sits down is closer to the person I am determined to be.

I always seek the most difficult situations in which to speak. I have spoken in San Bruno Prison to female inmates and in San Quentin; I have spoken to 150 deaf people when my talk was translated into sign language. (Speaking depends on timing and personality, which often do not get picked up by sign language.) I have spoken before 150 ten- to twelve-year-olds — that was the worst ever, because you never get their attention all at once, and they have different ideas of what is funny. One of my friends who accompanied me to this program thought it was a good experience for me because, as he said, "You're getting too used to people telling you you're good." That day I promised myself to accept any assignment that would help me grow as a person and as a speaker. So often we reach a competence level in our careers and are happy to coast. Many of the most dissatisfied people have accomplished major goals, and then didn't look for more opportunities. Grab any opportunity to develop beyond your present comfort barrier.

When that old "too comfortable" feeling creeps up on me, I get suspicious. It makes me scrutinize my life.

The "Secret" of Success

Ira Hayes, who for many years lectured for NCR Corporation as the company's "Ambassador of Enthusiasm" and who is now a famous speaker on his own, has told thousands of people his secrets of success. People have asked him, "Why do you stand up and tell your competition your secrets of success?" He answers, "Don't worry. It's difficult enough trying to get your *own* people to change. What makes you think the competition will do it?"

The same phenomenon in sharing secrets of success exists in the hairstyling business, for example, the idea of getting new customers to give you the names of six friends and then calling them, which I did early in my hairstyling career. It's scary because not everyone wants to come in. I used to call people up and say, "Don Collin is a client of mine and he suggested you might like to have your hair styled by me." Some people would say yes. And although I gave many of my first haircuts for free, sometimes people would still say no. But, a lot of people who did come in remained customers until I stopped hairstyling to devote all my time to public speaking. (Many of them are still good friends.)

Carole Kelby, a realtor, sold $15 million worth of homes in a supposedly poor market. From the time Carole entered the real estate business in 1974 until she became a top seller in 1979, most realtors were crying the blues. Because of her success in the real estate business, Carole was in great demand as a speaker. Five years later she became a full-time speaker and trainer. She made her commitment to be a full-time speaker when she was giving a talk to ophthalmologists on time management. She was speaking about making and then living up to commitments. A voice inside her said, "Practice what you preach!" So she suddenly announced, "At the end of next fall I will become a full-time speaker." On October 30 she did just that, giving up a large income to risk a new career.

One of Carole's greatest pleasures now is helping others be successful. One of her favorite classes has been with her former real estate company. She takes low- or no-production salespeople who are about to be fired or ready to quit, and feeds them on self-confidence. When they become confident, they start producing.

Carole got into the business because the real estate agent who was selling her home was impressed by her personality and suggested she'd make a good salesperson herself. Her secrets to success: she enjoys people, but she is very service-oriented; she lives the principle that my father explained to me, "Concentrate on being the type of person people want to do business with." She believes in honesty, sincerity, and integrity. She's a high achiever and did her best to find the perfect home for her clients.

Today, in addition to being a full-time speaker, she also owns an advertising specialty and card company. She seems excited about everything. "In my seminars," she says, "I tell everyone exactly what I do for success, but most people just won't do it. Why not? Either they fear failure or they fear success."

Avoid Being an Elephant

Human beings are like elephants. When a captive elephant is young, trainers put a chain around its ankle and attach the chain to a post. The elephant pulls and pulls and pulls, but can't escape. When the elephant is older the trainer ties a little rope from the elephant's leg to a small post in the ground. The elephant doesn't run away, though he is now strong enough to free himself. It is the same with people: They try something a few times, and if they aren't successful, they give up. Remember, none of us has forever to turn our life around. Time *is* our life; it's *all* we have.

Pregnancy and Women's Fear of Success

Some women will do anything to stay in the comfort zone — even something as uncomfortable as getting pregnant. According to Ruth Lawton, a feminist psychiatrist on the teaching staff of Columbia University, even highly talented women become pregnant to avoid anxiety over their blossoming careers. Characteristic, she says, is the case of an artist she knew who conceived accidentally, twice, five years apart. Each time she had been presented with an opportunity to do a one-woman show of her work, and each time she had gotten pregnant instead. As a result, her shows were put off until she was past fifty, vastly decreasing the time left for development and acknowledgment of her talents.

Looking over the roster of her patients in recent years, Dr. Lawton discovered she could easily count twenty women between the ages of forty and sixty who had used pregnancy as an escape from the outside world. In at least half of these cases, she noted, the third and fourth children were each conceived just when the other children were in school, leaving the mother free to devote more energy to work outside the home. Dr. Lawton calls this syndrome "compulsive child-rearing," by which she means mothering not for intrinsic gratification but as a substitute for action in the world.

President Matina Horner of Radcliffe College seems to agree. In an interview some years back, speaking of women's fear of success, she said she found that at the point women were closing the gap between their earnings and those of the significant male in their lives, many became pregnant in a strategic effort to avoid what they saw as an inevitable conflict.

We, the women of the world, and no doubt many men, have to work through this problem. When I opened my business I had a nervous stomach for two years. I have a nervous stomach sometimes even now, before many of my assignments.

Because today there are more than 2 million women in America making more money than their husbands, and because there are more jobs being created by entrepreneurial ventures than by corporations (and more women than men are initiating these ventures), the Cinderella complex may fade as a factor in keeping interested women out of the marketplace. A woman's place is wherever she wants to be.

What Else Comes with the Territory?

Each of us needs to work hard and feel uncomfortable. We know what Willie Loman thought was important in Arthur Miller's classic play, *Death of a Salesman*. But a smile and a shoeshine aren't the only things that come with the territory.

My father, Arthur Fripp, said that "some people catch the bus and some don't. You have a better chance of going places if you're in the waiting area when the bus arrives."

If you don't go out and do things, you'll remain forever fearful of the workings of the world. Go out and get the success. Get the experience. Participate.

YOUR ASSIGNMENT:
Overcoming Discomfort

Some things that make me uncomfortable are:

_____

_____

_____

Which of these things shall I "push against," to extend
my comfort zone?

_____

_____

_____

CHAPTER 5

Creativity Starts Young

> "Sir Joshua Reynolds, the great British portrait artist and master at producing subtle tones, was asked, 'What do you mix your colors with?' Sir Joshua replied, 'With brains.'
>
> You cannot plan creativity—you can only prepare the environment for it."
>
> O. A. Battista

A woman at a Credit Union National Association convention asked me where I got my degree in behavioral psychology. "Behind a hairstyling chair," I told her, " . . . a twenty-three-year degree." I have observed that many successful business people and entrepreneurs were always entrepreneurs. One millionaire in his forties told me that his first successful scheme, at age eight, was selling lizards and snakes. He had a great money-making venture until the city of Palo Alto closed him down. Today he runs many slightly more conventional businesses.

A successful life insurance salesman also discovered his selling ability at age eight. One winter in Shenandoah, Iowa, he arrived a bit late for his Cub Scout meeting. The leader of the den was explaining that the Scouts had to sell one hundred boxes of Christmas cards. The money would go to the church charity. Not realizing that the hundred boxes was the goal for the whole troop of Scouts, the boy trudged through the snow, knocking on doors every day after school, showing samples of cards, and collecting money. At the next Scout meeting, he was heartbroken to report that he had sold only ninety-eight boxes of cards. The leader stood in total disbelief—until the boy emptied the money from his pockets onto the table. (We often manage somehow to live up to what we think is demanded.)

While in college, the same boy developed a terrific business selling birthday cakes. He charged parents for the service, personalized the cakes, and delivered them to students. In a short period of time he had such a good business that he merely contacted the parents and had other students do all the leg work. As a young man he developed the habit of thinking creatively. No wonder he is a success today. (Lizards, snakes, and cakes aside, what was the idea that you had and never did anything about?)

Another client, one of the smartest, most successful business people I know, told me that when he was going to college he had a job working on roads. One day he was working very hard and he stopped to get a drink of water. He had not been goofing off; he had been giving his best, working harder than the men around him. The foreman suddenly shouted, "Don't be so lazy. Get back to work!" This man declared to himself then that he would never work for anyone else again.

When I was five, my younger brother and I participated in a ritual every Saturday night. We would stand before our parents in the kitchen, and our parents would ask, "What did you do this week to earn your pocket money?" For every good thing we did, we earned a penny. This experience encouraged me to think creatively. I thank my father for that early lesson which I remember as, "the harder you work and the more good things you do, the more you are rewarded."

As children, my brother and I frequently sold our used comic books by the front gate to earn extra money. But a twelve-year-old client, whom I met when I owned my salon, was even more enterprising than we were. Having overheard how quickly a friend had made $17, he took the friend's idea and expanded it. He borrowed initial set-up capital from his parents, purchased stencils, paint, and brushes, and practiced painting numbers. Then he called on neighbors and sold them on the idea of painting the house numbers on the curb outside their homes. To limit wasted time, he called prospects on the telephone at night. After quickly paying back the loan to his parents, he made a healthy profit.

This lad, a true entrepreneur, then subcontracted the work to his brother, who received a dollar less for performing the services. I commented to the father of this successful young man that his son impressed me because he always came up with fabulous money-making ideas. The father replied that although his children had a comfortable life because of his success, he did not lavish pocket money on them. In this way, they were encouraged to be imaginative. I myself have noticed that not giving too much to children encourages them to make more of themselves. (I have always maintained that one of the best things we can do for children is to teach them the value of money. Recently at a Bank of America awards program, a self-made multimillionaire disagreed. He said, "It's not *one* of the best things, it's *the* best thing parents can do.")

The Benefit of Sibling Rivalry

Probably the best thing that ever happened to me was growing up with a brilliant brother only one year younger than I. He was always at the top of his class, and I was always somewhere near the middle, so I got the impression that I was not as smart as others. I never missed school for fear that I would get behind. Although I didn't win anything else, I had perfect attendance certificates for years. One day in my middle twenties, I realized what had happened. I looked around to see whether I was still keeping up and discovered that everyone else was miles behind.

How did this happen? I had developed good work habits. On Tuesday evenings, during my hairstyling apprenticeship, all the students would practice by doing models' hair. The other students would work on one or two models. I would always do five. Many evenings I also would practice on my neighbors' hair. Then, at the age of eighteen, I left home and went to live on an island off the coast of France. There I worked in a salon with some sophisticated gentlemen from the west end of London. They could do hairstyles that I had never even seen before, but they believed that lunch hours were for eating lunch. I believed lunch hours were for squeezing three extra customers in. One day my boss told me that I actually produced 30 percent more income for the salon than the guys who were more talented, just by doing more.

When I arrived in San Francisco and worked at the Mark Hopkins Hotel, my boss had never seen anyone work like me. He said, "Patricia, will you go back to England and bring over twenty-four of your friends?"

"I don't know twenty-four people in England who work like me," I replied.

As Calvin Coolidge wrote, "Nothing in the world can take the place of persistence. Talent will not, genius will not, and education will not." What happened was that I developed the habit of not "goofing off." Persistence, determination, and hard work made the difference for me. As the modern-day philosopher Woody Allen said, "Eighty percent of life is just turning up."

Ideas from Bright Young Executives

The successful owner of a financial investment company, someone I know well in San Francisco, went to work right out of college for a major airline. Soon he was a young executive, up-and-coming, bright, and with good ideas. One day he had an idea about saving money for the company. At the time, the executives who had the biggest budgets were paid more and had more power. He convinced the company that instead of rewarding people for spending more money and controlling bigger budgets, it should reward people for saving money. His idea made that company a million dollars. The idea was just common sense and he thought, "Well, here I am, a young kid in this big, powerful company and I just had an idea that saved them a million dollars. I got a $200-a-month raise. I knew at that moment I could do better on my own."

The important thing is not how bright this young man was—his brainstorm evolved from common sense—or how much money he actually saved a huge corporation, but his habit of thinking creatively. He had planned a career with a large company but chucked everything and moved to California, because, as he figured, "If I'm going to do what I'm doing, I can do it anywhere, and I'd rather live in California." The point is, you can start anywhere from scratch, but the "scratch" begins with the thinking process—about where you are and where it is you want to be.

"Who Are the DeBolts?"

One of the most inspiring stories about young people is one you may have read about or seen on television or film, one of the most amazing families I know—the DeBolts. Dorothy and her first husband had five children and were so happy they wanted to share their joy. They adopted two more children—all handicapped (or "physically challenged" as they prefer to say). Then her husband died and she was left as a single parent. As a widow she adopted two war-wounded Vietnamese children.

She then met Bob DeBolt, successful president of a prestigious San Francisco building firm. They fell in love, and he brought his one daughter into the family, bringing their family to ten. After their marriage they adopted ten more multiple-handicapped, multiracial children. The children would walk to school in the affluent neighborhood of Piedmont, and refused rides from neighbors because they were so proud that they could manage on their own. Soon the able-bodied children of the neighborhood followed their example.

For Christmas the gifts they gave each other were unique: They set and reached major accomplishments, such as climbing stairs on crutches. Early in their marriage Bob resigned from his very good job to help Dorothy found and lead AASK (Aid to Adoption of Special Kids), a national non-profit adoption organization which has now placed thousands of special needs children into adoptive families.

Bob and Dorothy are very popular on the lecture circuit. Their talks are full of stories of how these exceptional young people are a living example to us all of creativity, persistence and teamwork. Today all of the children are living on their own and working to pay for their own college educations.

When asked how their life has changed since the kids have left home, Bob replied that now they can run naked through the house. Dorothy reminded him that they could do that when the last child was at home because he was blind. When audiences hear the wit and wisdom and true stories of this exceptional family, it is impossible for them not to be inspired to do better themselves.

YOUR ASSIGNMENT:
Creativity

Some great ideas that I've never followed up on are:

The one I select to follow up on now is:

And to do it, I'm going to:

My time frame will be:

CHAPTER 6

Procrastination

"Do it from inspiration, not desperation."

E. James Rohn

One of the biggest reasons people are not successful is because they procrastinate. And one of the biggest reasons people procrastinate is because they are afraid of making mistakes.

But here's the news: The only people who don't make mistakes are those who don't attempt anything. Often the worst mistake you can make is not doing something—anything! Shakespeare, that master cliché-coiner, spoke of the "tide in the affairs of man which, taken at the flood, leads on to fortune; omitted, all the voyage of their life is bound in shallows and in miseries." Sitting tight because you are afraid to move is as pointless as racing about just to be doing something.

Waiting . . . and Waiting

A woman came up to me after a speech I gave about "Decisions That Can Turn Your Life Around." She said, "I realize I have been putting off doing things since my husband died. I was waiting until I lost weight and I was waiting until this occurred or that happened." The reasons for waiting seem to make sense at the time, but they are just excuses. Soon waiting becomes a bad habit, a way of life.

Dr. Dru Scott talks about what she calls "for best"—how at home the family silver was always kept "for best." The family silver was too good for Friday night's Kentucky Fried Chicken or Wednesday night's spaghetti. Her father died, and then her mother had a stroke, and Dru looked after her. Though it was a struggle for her to talk, Dru's mother took her hand and said, "Take out the best silver. 'For best' is now."

People are always waiting. "I won't buy new clothes or try to meet new people until I lose weight," they decide, or "I won't do this until the children go to school," "I won't start that until the children have left home," or "I won't do this until I get a divorce" (or "until I get married").

If you want to do something, *do it now*.

In Four Years . . .

There is a story about a thirty-seven-year-old man who says, "Well, I'd like to go to college, but by the time I get out, I'd be forty-one." His friend replies, "Well how old will you be in four years if you *don't* go to college?"

One woman told me after a college lecture that a friend had suggested she come to hear me speak. "I was a little concerned," the woman continued, "because no one was going to come with me. But I'm glad I came. When I went back to school—I had been recently divorced and I had to go to school to learn how to do something—I was really scared." At forty she thought everyone would be younger and smarter than she was, and she didn't want to be shown up. Her friends kept asking, "What if you flunk out?—What if you don't do well?" "'Hell,' I said to myself, 'I'll give it a try.' Now I couldn't be happier."

After one of the first talks I ever gave, a woman approached me. She too had been putting off doing things. "At this rate," she said, "I realize I'm never going to do *anything*. I want to turn my life around. How do I get started?" I told her to take a Dale Carnegie course and to start forcing herself to get involved. Once you have successful experiences, it gets easier to try new things. But you've got to take those few first risks. (I have never worked for the Dale Carnegie organization, but I recommend the company for its success in helping people acquire skills and self-confidence, as well as for the quality of people you meet.)

Limiting Yourself

There's the old story of the freshwater fisherman who was amazed to note that another fisherman just upstream consistently measured his catches, keeping only the smallest of the lot and tossing the ten-inch, eleven-inch and twelve-inch prizes back into the water. Finally, the first fisherman asked the other, "Why are you throwing away the biggest and the best fish? I can't take any fish over nine inches home," the man replied, "because I have only a nine-inch frying pan."

Often, that's how we react in our daily lives, thinking that the biggest jobs and the best opportunities we face are simply too overwhelming. Yet, completing a difficult task is simply a matter of fitting the fish to the pan by cutting it into pieces. Similarly, achieving our goals is easy once we've planned each step carefully, and then tackle each step one at a time. If you set up challenging yet attainable goals, detail each step you must achieve along the route, and take the goals one at a time, you'll never — to return to our fish story — toss a prize fish back into the river again.

Procrastination Can Be a Pain

Once I had to fire a new employee. This man — I will call him Bob — talked a good game, but he was unreliable, unprofessional, dishonest, and everything else no one wants in an employee. My experiences with him had been causing me no little anguish. One day I was out with my friend Camille. At the time I was in pretty good physical shape except for recurring neck and shoulder pains that I couldn't understand. (I too had mistakenly believed that stress had nothing to do with physical ailments.)

Camille was intrigued. Her husband, who was also under pressure, was having similar pains. "Patricia," she said, "it sounds like working with Bob is making you sick." I suddenly realized she was right. I don't know why it had taken me so long, but I said to myself, "I'm in charge of hiring and firing. I hired him — I can fire him." That was on Wednesday. I decided to fire him on Saturday because he had appointments the rest of the week.

That night I was with another friend, John, and I was telling him I was starting to feel better than I'd felt in weeks. "I've decided to fire a troublesome employee on Saturday," I explained. "Patricia," John said, "fire him tomorrow." It hadn't even occurred to me to cancel Bob's appointments or have someone else take them over.

The next day Bob called in late again. I said, "I need you here now. I need to talk to you." He came in and quit because he suspected what was about to happen, giving notice as of the following Sunday. I said, "No, I want you out of here in one hour." My pain in the neck was gone.

Procrastination As Birth Control

In her book, *Free Yourself to Write*, San Francisco therapist Joan Minninger tells about the woman who came to her with a writing block that was keeping her from getting her degree. She had procrastinated about writing her thesis until she was in danger of missing the deadline and losing credits toward her degree. As she and Joan explored some possible causes, Joan learned that the woman and her husband were waiting to have children until after the thesis was finished.

"How do you feel about having a baby?" Joan asked. The woman was very ambivalent. Joan's cure for the woman's procrastination consisted of persuading her that writing a thesis and having a baby were two separate issues. "She had discovered an entirely new form of birth control!" Joan says.

In some cases, Joan says, people use procrastination as a subconscious protective measure — often obsolete, usually illogical, and almost never effective as a long-term solution because it doesn't address the real problem. We develop protective patterns and then continue to use them long after they stop being useful. She suggests that you ask yourself:

☆ What am I protecting myself from?
☆ How is what I am doing helpful?
☆ Do I still need to protect myself this way?
☆ Am I ready to discard this behavior because I don't need it any more?

The Day That Changes Everything

Once you make a decision about a nagging problem, you feel better. You give things a chance to fall into place. Your energies become centered. And when you have some direction, you naturally feel better. When I decided to end a frustrating situation and fire Bob, I felt better. After two days, I eliminated the pain in my neck, the pain in my shoulder — and the pain in my life.

One of my favorite speakers, Jim Rohn, gives a section of his talk called "The day that turns your life around." There comes a day, he maintains, when you just say, "I'm not going to put up with this anymore." That's the day you stop procrastinating.

It's Never Too Late

"When I was fifty-eight years old," said the late Doug Hooper at age sixty-four, "two things happened to change my whole life. First of all, I decided to discard a lot of things. I gave up a lot of beliefs I had tenaciously been holding on to about myself all my life. These were beliefs about my own limits. So many of us go through life, particularly when we get older, using the two most dreaded words of all, *if only*. We say, 'If only I had a better childhood, or more education, or a different wife, or a different husband.' My personal 'if only' was 'if only I had more education.' I stopped at high school and was conditioned to believe that if you don't go to college, you lead a mediocre life. I believed it and *for that reason it was true*.

"Finally I decided the time had come to discard those false beliefs. About twenty years ago, through a strange series of events, I started going into the prisons of California and teaching a philosophy that I hadn't really lived up to myself: that people could change their attitudes and their thinking, and have a better life. When I began seeing the tremendous changes in some of these men, I decided to try some of these principles in my own life.

"The other thing I did — and this can change the life of anybody willing to do it — was to pledge that any time anything at all came up in my life that could possibly be for my own improvement or for someone else's, I would say 'yes' — immediately. Let me emphasize that word *immediately*, because if you don't say 'yes' quickly, if you give yourself time to think about it, you end up saying 'no'!

"I remembered that pledge to myself," Hooper continued, "when I blurted out 'yes' to an invitation to speak to the Contra Costa (California) Board of Realtors and, boy, I sure wished I hadn't, especially as the time to speak drew nearer. However, that one talk changed my life because it went over very well. I was then asked to give a talk the following week to the Kiwanis Club. The editor of the local paper, the *Contra Costa Times*, with a circulation of about one hundred thousand, happened to be present that day. He and I talked afterward about my philosophy and some of my experiences in the prisons. All of a sudden, out of the clear sky — I'd never written anything in my life — I said, 'Maybe I can put some of these things in a weekly column for you.'

"The chance of getting a column in the paper, when you've never written anything, isn't very good, but he said, 'Strange you should happen to suggest that. I just canceled a column this morning and I was wondering how I could fill it for a while. Do you think you could put together perhaps a dozen columns? That would give a little continuity and give me a chance to replace it later.' I said, 'I don't know if I could write a dozen or not, but I'll start.'"

At the time Doug Hooper died, column number 300 had been published, and his columns reached nearly 2 million homes in syndication. A collection of Hooper's columns was published by Prentice-Hall. Hooper's strong message resulted in invitations to lecture, which he did as a profession. "Imagine if I'd said 'no' to that first invitation to talk," he often mused. "The point is, say 'yes' immediately; don't stop to think about it."

Don't Get Robbed

My countryman Samuel Johnson (the literary light of the eighteenth century) once said, "Procrastination is the thief of time." It's about time that each of us incarcerates that thief for life.

YOUR ASSIGNMENT:
Start Starting

Some things I often procrastinate about are:

My choices for action are:

My action plan is:

CHAPTER 7

Cinderella's Complex—And Ours

*"We only have one real shot at liberation and
that is to emancipate ourselves from within."*

Colette Dowling,
The Cinderella Complex

The Cinderella Complex, a thoughtful and intelligent book by Colette Dowling, penetrates the core of the dilemma many women face today. "Women," she writes, "have been encouraged since they were children to be dependent to an unhealthy degree. Any woman who looks within knows that she has been trained to feel comfortable with the idea of not taking care of herself or asserting herself. At best, we may have played the game of independence, inwardly envying the boys and later the men because they seemed so naturally self-sufficient." By contrast, Dowling says, men learn that they are their own saviors.

Dowling believes that "it is not nature that bestows the self-sufficiency on men. Males are educated in independence from the day they are born. Just as systematically, females are taught that they have an out, that some day in some way they are going to be saved. This is the fairy tale . . . only hang on long enough, the childhood story goes, and some day, somebody will come along to rescue you from the anxiety of authentic living. . . ."

Happily Ever After

I seem to have been luckier than many people. My mother brought me up to think that marriage (my parents were happily married for forty-five years) is great, but not "all it's cracked up to be." She urged me to have lots of boyfriends so that I would be able to make intelligent choices: "Marriage is not everything it's cracked up to be. Marriage is not what the fairy tales lead us to believe."

More than ever, being your own person and having your own career can make life easier in the long run. This applies, of course, to both men and women. I feel deeply for people who suddenly, through a spouse's death or departure or through their own feelings, wake up alone believing they have no choices. There is an aching irony here. So many people get married because they are afraid to be alone, but divorce statistics show that marriage is not a guarantee that you will have company and support when you grow older. *Learn to fend for yourself.* Have something you do well — something that makes you feel good, that gives you self-esteem. Then you can handle a lot of other problems.

Dowling admits that she herself did not want the stress involved in being responsible for her own welfare. On an unconscious level, she felt it was appropriate that her male companion work harder and take more risks "simply because he was a man." Worse, she confesses, "I always felt there was something not entirely feminine about a real commitment to work, as if I would become something less than womanly if I were to really get out there and dig and haul in the common market of the adult economy." Sad to say, this feeling is shared by many women despite the fact that more women than ever make up the work force.

Money and Freedom

As a young woman, I loved going to tea with my mother and her friends. As an apprentice hairdresser in my mid-teens, I would go to lunch with my mother on Thursday when my father was at Rotary. It was very elegant and lady-like, an appropriate activity for women who don't have to work. But I never minded working. I always wanted the opportunity to work, and I always liked having money. I could not wait to grow up and have the money to treat my mother. Today, both feeling we are affluent, we fight to see who pays for what! But many women are caught, as Dowling writes, "hopelessly enmeshed in this neurotic double bind of hating and fearing both dependence and independence simultaneously."

For an article in the early 1970s I was asked what were husbands' biggest complaints about their wives. I said that many husbands complained that their wives had no idea what it took to make money — that they wanted their husbands to make $60,000 a year and be home at five o'clock. Another complaint was that the wife's entire life revolved around her husband, which created too great a responsibility for the man.

Marriage and Fulfillment

Many people used to be programmed to believe that in order to be successful, to be fulfilled as an individual, one had to be married. Later they found out this was not necessarily true. People change as they grow older. A person who considers marrying young needs to ask, "Do I want to be married?" If the answer is "yes," the next question is "What compromises am I prepared to continue making?" (I feel fortunate indeed that my mother never programmed me to think I would be unsuccessful if I did not marry.)

One problem, psychologist Dru Scott suggests, may be that many women have problems thinking about what they want for themselves because for many years it was the husband first or the children first. They never realize it's okay to want something. It's quite all right to want anything in the world as long as it doesn't hurt someone else. Any relationship is doomed unless people are together because they choose to be together and not solely because they feel a need for another person.

The important thing is that people should have something in their life — be it a job, a hobby, a charity, whatever — where they don't need anyone else involved to feel fulfilled. Problems arise when people allow their lives to revolve too much around someone else. If that person dies, or leaves, they are devastated. (One thing about being single is that, not having someone else who is responsible for you, you have to go out and do things on your own.)

"I Can Do It"

Independence, as Colette Dowling points out, stems from a realization that we can accomplish a task on our own. However, many women fail to acquire the confidence that comes from performing well in competitive situations. The notion that women cannot succeed on their own creeps in and sits silently in the corner until it is accepted as a fixture, a given, something venerable and ultimately unassailable. The result of this acceptance shows up throughout a woman's life.

While helping to coach the women's basketball team at the college where he taught, Dick Friedrich, professor of English, observed this phenomenon. "It was fascinating for me to see how the psychological and physical oppression of women takes place. We can see how they practice what they have been taught about athletics and excellence in competition. A good deal of what men have been taught about themselves, how they can get better, and how they can learn, just hasn't been a part of the women's education. It has been enough that women could play basketball without breaking their fingers — they have not been expected to do well, to excel. It's been enough for them to play at all.

"Women *do* learn. They haven't been taught to pretend they know it all, as men have. When you try to teach women something, if you can get them to practice it through their initial expected failures, they learn it. They *do* progress, and it's fun to watch."

The Role of Role Models

Without role models, we'd all still be sitting about in caves. One woman who provided a role model for me was Mary, owner of a highly successful laundry in San Francisco. When I first met Mary, I was twenty and she was forty. She was the only businesswoman I really knew when I first came to California. She was beautiful, always dressed well, and lived in an enormous and lovely condominium. Seeing her, I wasn't envious, but I thought, "If she can do it, so can I." Like supportive employees and friends, a role model provides incentive.

One day when I had turned forty, I bumped into Mary on the street and we made a lunch date. It was so nice to be a grown-up person and take her, my role model, out to lunch. To my surprise and pleasure, Mary told me she had read about my progress and had been sure I wouldn't "end up behind a chair." She said, "Once at my hairdresser's they were talking about you, so my ears pricked up. They said, 'Patricia Fripp doesn't take time for lunch — she doesn't even take time to go to the bathroom.' I was so amused because that was how I built my business, by wasting no time and eating my lunch at my desk."

The first time I discovered I was providing a similar incentive was when a young woman approached me and said, "I always try to emulate you. I bought a Dale Carnegie book because you recommended it. Carnegie said, 'Don't try to be like anyone else; just try to be like you.' Then I understood what you've been telling us — not to be like anyone else, but to make the most of ourselves."

At that moment, I realized how important it is for women to have other women whom they can admire. Even though I no longer run a hairstyling business, I always try to provide role models for small entrepreneurs, especially women, who are entering the business world. Every businesswoman has this responsibility, to provide an incentive for other women to succeed.

Alone at Last

In the final analysis, we each have to succeed on our own. Reverberating in my mind is Ralph Waldo Emerson's declaration that "nothing is at last sacred but the integrity of your own mind."

Today more jobs are being created by entrepreneurs than by corporations, and more women are starting those jobs. Many women entrepreneurs are concerned about their roles as women in the business world, traditionally a man's domain. In a radio interview, I was asked by a feminist friend, Suzy Sutton, why I like to be called Miss. I facetiously replied, "To let the world know I'm single and available. Also," I explained, "I have built a business and a name for myself, and I have done it alone. I want people to be aware that I alone have done it. I'm very proud of that accomplishment."

Who Is the Enemy?

Men are not the enemy. I would not have succeeded in my speaking career or my hairstyling business without the support of many people, both men and women. Although some men (and women) still operate under obsolete rules, there are many who do not. It is true that in the past women have been repressed by laws and attitudes that sought to "protect" them, but that is changing. A hundred years ago the New York City YMCA first instituted women's typing classes in the face of widespread opposition. At the time, people claimed that women could never stand up to such stress. Needless to say, women have disproved that theory.

Overcoming Prejudice

Obstacles continue. At the beginning of my career as a men's hairstylist, I had the opportunity to work with the fabulous Jay Sebring, hairstylist to many movie stars and other well-known people. Although he was a brilliant publicity man and a great hairstylist, Jay was also a bit of a chauvinist. At the time, few women were in men's hairstyling, and I had to work twice as hard as the men in the shop to prove to Jay that I was worth training. My efforts were not in vain, however, because Jay noticed my work and kept me as an apprentice.

One weekend, as he was about to fly to Los Angeles, Jay shook my hand and said, "Patricia, you are really doing great haircuts." It was tremendously exciting to have proven myself to my teacher, one of the greats in the business.

That same weekend, in Los Angeles, Jay Sebring was murdered, a victim of the Manson family massacre. I was devastated, but determined to remember everything he had tried so hard to teach me. Among other things, dealing with Jay taught me not to let male chauvinism or any other type of prejudice get in my way. Life just isn't long enough for that.

A lot has changed. A lot hasn't. All of us — men as well as women — must somehow come to terms with both the overt and covert barriers women face. Now, many working women complain about the lack of opportunity and the prejudice against which they must battle. Rather than complain, we need to spend our energy being twice as good as we have to be. The only way things will change is if attitudes change, and it is up to the working women to make everyone, including themselves, realize that they are a professional class.

Since I came to America and began working, I have used the "disadvantage" of being a woman to my own good. Working in a predominantly male profession, men's hairstyling, I at first stood out as a woman. People who came to see me were surprised to see that "Pat" was female. "Women can't cut men's hair — can they?" some customers would ask. And, of course, once I had done their hair, they returned, both for the novelty of a woman barber and for a good haircut. (The former without the latter wouldn't have lasted, nor should it.) Now, in the men's hairstyling world, women have literally taken over. Long before I retired from the business, more than 70 percent of the students in barber school were women.

You will find that many people have prejudices against others for many different reasons: They are too fat, too thin, black, white, yellow, not good-looking enough, or even too handsome. You are not going to change them. Life isn't particularly fair, and that's the way it is. The trick is to turn the prejudice around. Say to yourself, "Okay, I'm not crazy about this problem, but how am I going to adapt to make it work *for* me?"

Ten years ago some companies believed women speakers could not know much about management or sales. Today being a woman is an advantage. Women are making major strides in corporations, and many companies and industries that are still male-dominated want to prove they are forward-thinking by hiring women speakers.

Solving the Mystery

Perhaps women only need to demystify the male domain. Sometimes a close look is enough to do the job. Terry Helms, who started at one company as a typist earning $500 a month, got the glimpse she needed. She had a superb boss who sent her through a sales training class so that she could learn the business and be more effective. "It took me two and a half years," Terry says, "to realize I knew as much as they did, if not more. They were making lots of money. I finally told my boss I had to get into sales even though it scared me half to death." (When I met her she was making a very substantial six-figure income.)

Another woman, with Pacific Telesis, told me, "As I became involved in jobs where I had more and more exposure to higher and higher levels of management—third, fourth, fifth levels of management, all male bastions—I saw the way men performed. I thought, 'I can do what they're doing. Some of it better.' I think it took exposure to those levels, and seeing how men performed, to recognize it."

This woman is passing the lesson on: "I tell my children—one boy, one girl—that they can achieve anything they want to achieve, that it's up to them. But there's a lot of other conditioning out there. I try not to get too much into sexism because I don't want them to be too conscious of it. Instead, I just say to both of them, 'Look, you have potential and you can do anything you want to do. It's up to you—unless you're physically restrained from doing it.' I want them to know they can choose."

When Crisis Strikes

We all want to be able to choose, but it doesn't always happen that way. It didn't for Venita VanCaspel. "I was happily married," Venita says, "when one day my husband took a business trip on the Braniff Electra. The wing fell off and everyone was killed. For a while I said, 'Why? Why?' We were clean, went to church, and did all those beautiful things, and I kept saying, 'Why, Lord?' But when I finally discovered that I could not have the answer, I quit asking. Next, I went through a period when I said, 'Lord, there must be a reason you left me here alone with so much of my life still ahead of me. You must have a blueprint for me. Just show me what the blueprint is and I'll do it.'

"But that's not the way the Lord works either; he doesn't lay out a blueprint for us to see. I began to feel that as I took one step, I would know the next step, like going down a pathway at night with a lantern.

You can't see the end of the path, but if you take the next step you can see to take the next step, and the next step. Finally, you arrive at where you should be.

"And this was the way it was with me. I kept taking the next step. I had received some life insurance upon the death of my husband. I had a degree in economics and a degree in finance — a lot more education than the average woman had at that time — yet I hadn't been taught what to do with money. So I went back to college and all I did was study investments. I learned what to do with my own money. All that time I was searching for something worthwhile to do with my life.

"I decided to be a stockbroker. That seems simple enough, but in 1961 in Houston, Texas, it wasn't. A woman stockbroker? No such luck. I went from firm to firm to firm, and they all said, 'We tried a woman once and it didn't work.' Of course, men also dropped out daily without being singled out by sex. I finally got out the rules of the New York Stock Exchange and read them. You would be amazed at what they said. They said you had to work for a member firm six months and pass the test. Period. That's all the rules said. So I got a job in the back office of a brokerage firm and I sent off for a correspondence course. I studied the Exchange rules. At the end of the six months, I told the firm where I worked that I'd like to take the examination. They called me a crackpot. I said again that I'd like to take the exam. Thinking I couldn't pass it, they finally said, 'All right.' I took it and I passed.

"Then the brokerage firm had a bigger problem: what to do with me. I remember the boss calling me in. He cleared his throat and he said, 'I think we'll throw you in the water and see if you can swim. I'll tell you what that means. It means we carry the men on a draw (give them a salary) for a year, but we're not going to give you any money. If you need anything, ask for it.' That was my training program. You know, you *can* learn to swim — if you just have the courage to hop in the water."

Isn't it high time some of us began putting on our swimsuits?

The Successful Woman: How Is She Different?

A 1983 study by Luann Lindquist, Ph.D., focuses on successful career women and how they balance two essential aspects of their lives: love and work. Says Lindquist, "Sigmund Freud said that our challenge as human beings is to have a life in which work and personal relationships have balance." Lindquist studied fifty-four women to determine how they achieved "the ideal," success with relationships and money. She chose earned income as one of the criteria for success. Her subjects had to earn between $50,000 and $200,000 a year. They also had to be between the ages of thirty-five and fifty-five and are or have been involved in a relationship with a man. (Her study concentrated on heterosexual relationships.)

Lindquist studied these women to find out what it was they did and how they did it. "One trait common to every woman was that, no matter how successful they had become or how deep their personal relationships were, each said she would never give up her career.

"Most of the time people say, 'Well, I'm just gonna make a bunch of money and retire.' However, these women knew that work was an essential part of their lives, that their sense of self grew out of what they did. They made a strong commitment to their career. They could always find a partner. Now, not all of them were with a man at the time, but they were more satisfied with their life than the general population; they were more satisfied with their relationships and they felt better about themselves than any other group."

Some of these women had lost men who couldn't han-dle the success of their partners. Lindquist asked her subjects, "What is the price you pay for success?" Every woman surveyed replied in various ways that they had given up *poor* personal and professional relationships, as well as low self-esteem. "I gave up thinking that I couldn't do this or that," they would say, "and I learned how to take a lot of risks." The risks included losing friendships and exposing themselves to the possibility of failure.

Lindquist found that her subjects didn't fear success — on their way up the success ladder they were going for it — but they did fear losing relationships. "Women are more relationship-oriented than men. Their concern is if I do this, or if I go back to school or for special training or start traveling more, what is this going to do with my relationship?" She feels that Matina Horner's 1968 University of Michigan study on sex differences in achievement, motivation, and performance (written up as "Fail: Bright Women" in *Psychology Today*) was valid then, but not today.

Lindquist believes that the successful career woman today is determined not to be "stressed out" by her job or to give up personal relationships entirely. As a therapist, Lindquist deals with men who are trying to relate to a wife who has changed dramatically since they married. Twenty years ago this man married a nice, unassertive young woman who then decided she wants to go out and make it in the world. Now she has.

"It's the woman in the couple that I work with more," Lindquist says, "because she's the one who has to change her thinking about things like delegating housework, baking the cookies for the kids, somebody else doing the shopping and the gardening — all those things she thinks she should be doing because she's a female." Men rarely have difficulty delegating, but women identify tasks with biology, with being a Woman.

"Many women have difficulty even saying to the men in their lives, 'Would you shop for dinner tonight?' or 'Would you straighten up the bathroom before everybody comes?' It isn't the men who are saying, 'Make sure all of that stuff's done, and I'll be happy.' That's not what I hear. I have found that women do not want to give up their control over what they see as female. But once women suggest they need help, the men take up the chores, like changing the bed or washing the dishes. They work things out."

When Lindquist goes into a corporation as an advisor on employee relations, she finds that communications are the biggest problem: "It may seem trite, but communications are as important in business as in personal relationships — 'what's right' versus 'who's right,' a matter of getting egos out of the way, making sure of the purpose. Why are these people together? You have to reestablish why they got together in the first place, what kinds of changes have been made, how they have developed over the years. Agreeing on purpose lets the purpose be fulfilled."

YOUR ASSIGNMENT:
Abandoning Fairy Tales and Myths

An obsolete attitude I still have about male/female relationships that gets in my way is:

This myth is no longer useful because:

I [ ] choose [ ] don't choose to discard it.

CHAPTER 8

Self-Image and Confidence

"You can have anything you want in life if you dress for it."

Edith Head,
Hollywood costume designer

"One thing you should know about me is that I'm stupid," Arthur L. Schawlow, 1981 Nobel Prize winner, told an astonished class of undergraduates at the University of California, Berkeley. "But lots of other people are stupid, too," he continued, "which is kind of nice. It means they miss a lot of things. If you can discover one of the things they've missed, you may win a Nobel Prize too."

You can bet that those students left that room with increased confidence in their own ability to make a difference in the world.

Seeing Yourself

"When people see themselves—really see themselves—they see what they are capable of becoming," insists Bert Decker of Decker Communications, the fastest-growing communications training organization in the country. "People's inadequacies are much greater in their own minds than in anybody else's," he emphasizes.

"For instance, when people hear themselves on audiotape, they say, 'Whose voice is that? It doesn't sound like me.' People think they come across worse than they actually do. And the first time they see themselves on video, they're in shock. But after once, twice, three times, they begin looking at themselves objectively and they think, 'Hey, nobody can see my knees shaking, my butterflies fluttering. Nobody can see what I did behind the barn ten years ago or all the inadequacies I have because my mother told me to be all the things that I'm not.'

"A sixty-year-old woman came in," says Decker. "She worked for her son and he sent her. She was a rather meek housewife type, dominated by her husband. Her son ran a string of successful insurance companies. She managed one of his small offices in Los Angeles and did some selling on the telephone, but she didn't like it because she was shy.

"Her son, who had taken our video-feedback communications course, sent all his people through it. She came in, saw the lights and the cameras, and thought it was a seminar, a lecture where somebody else was about to speak. When she realized she would be speaking, she became terrified, but she had guts enough to get up there the first time and talk about herself. She was frightened, believe me, and after she saw herself, she was traumatized. She felt as if she looked thirty years older than her sixty years.

"But at the end of two days, she announced, 'We were supposed to hire someone to sell while I ran the office, but I'm going back to do the selling and we'll hire somebody else to run the office.' This was a woman who had spoken in public three times in her life, two of which were toasts at weddings."

Fortunate Beginnings

Simon Cameron, Secretary of War under President Lincoln, was once asked why his son—who was smart, attractive, and had all the advantages of his father's influence and prestige—had not done as well as his father had in politics. "Donald is a likely fellow and would do well," Cameron replied, "but you must remember that I started life with a big advantage over him—poverty!"

Like Cameron's son, many of us have not had a beginning that forced us to face life positively. It then becomes important to seek out positive reinforcement and to concentrate on our better qualities. Even in a profession like hairstyling which focuses primarily on self-improvement, I have encountered haircutters with a poor self-image. I encouraged them to realize how important they can be in influencing lives.

What are you doing that's positive, life-enhancing, even indispensable? You can't do a really fine job at anything if you don't feel the importance of it.

Saying "Yes" to Yourself

Saying "yes" to yourself means acknowledging what you have that's good and working on the things that aren't. At one of my speaking engagements not too long ago, I had the good fortune to meet Nina Fortin, a superb example of someone who said "yes".

When Nina was nine years old, in Italy during World War II, she was standing outside her grandmother's store. A twenty-four- year-old American soldier came over to her, took her by the hand, and asked to meet her parents. When he met them, they exchanged addresses and he said, "This is the cleanest little girl in town." Three years later, when Nina was twelve, her parents received a note from the American asking whether he could marry her when she grew up. When Nina was fifteen, her mother died and she had to help raise her younger brothers and sisters, the youngest was only eleven months old.

Two years later the American soldier returned to Italy to marry Nina. Her father told her that she could probably not do any better — that he was probably a rich American, that she should marry him and go to America. She did.

In America, though she could not speak one word of English, she went to work in a factory near Cleveland. For the first year of her marriage, Nina couldn't even talk to her husband. Later they moved to California and she got a job cleaning model homes for a real estate company. One of the agents showing a house said, "Nina, why don't you get a real estate license and sell real estate?" She replied, "Well, not only can I not read English, but because Mussolini closed the schools during the war, I've had only two years of education in my own language."

Nina talked to her husband about the agent's suggestion. Her husband was unsupportive, but after many days of thinking, she told him, "If you will not buy some sort of insurance policy that absolutely guarantees that I am totally looked after if you die, then I must be my own insurance policy."

So Nina went to school to get a real estate license. It wasn't easy for her. (One day she asked the teacher, "What is that pimple?" He said, "What pimple?" It was a decimal point, and she did not know what it was or what it was called.) But her teacher was very sympathetic and helped her.

After she got her license, she went on to get a broker's license, which requires a more complicated test than a real estate license. The first time she took the brokers' exam, she missed passing by one and a half points. The second time, she passed. "I was taking this exam with really educated people, CPAs, lawyers," she explained. She met one CPA the first time she took the exam. It was the ninth time he'd taken it and failed. He had to take it ten times before he passed. "How come you got it on the second try and it took me ten times?" the CPA later asked.

"Because I'm ignorant," she told him. "And because I'm ignorant, I listen to what the teacher says and I do what he tells me. Because you are so smart, you have to argue every point. You may debate well, but I think you are more interested in showing off to the class."

She learned to pass the test because she knew something about life. Sometimes smart people outsmart themselves. It's an old story: When you don't have an education, you're forced to use your brain. Obstacles and limitations—even severe ones—can be overcome.

Life magazine published a story about Nina Fortin's life—a story well worth remembering. In 1987 I met Nina again at a convention in Las Vegas. She's still doing exceptionally well.

Above-Average Human Beings

As we strive to improve ourselves, we should emphasize our accomplishments rather than our failures. Several years ago at a self-improvement seminar in San Francisco, the seminar leader asked the group of 350 how many of them thought they were above average. My hand shot up. Then he asked, "How many of you think you are below average?" A few people put their hands up.

"Well," he continued, "how many of you think you are in the lowest one-third of the people?" I couldn't believe anyone at a self-improvement seminar could honestly believe he or she fell within the lowest one-third of all people. But one tiny woman in the back row put up her hand. The leader ran back to her and said, "How could you possibly believe you are in the lowest one-third of all people?" She said, "You don't understand. I can't read or write very well."

This woman had come over from Italy twenty-nine years before. She had traveled widely in Europe and America, and she spoke three languages fluently. She had a good knowledge of American history because she had studied to become a citizen, and on her own she had raised three children. All three were successful in college. This woman had held the same job as a waitress for eleven years, and she owned her own home (paid for free and clear). She had $5,000 in the bank. But, you understand, she couldn't read or write very well. The seminar leader then discussed the different areas of her life, and "graded" her on each. "Well," he said, "we have to give you 100 percent for being a good mother. . . ." On he went rating each area of the woman's life. On reading and writing she got a zero. At the end she was, on the leader's scale, an all-round 72-percent person—surely above average.

Attitude or Education?

No matter how good we look or how sophisticated we are, too often we concentrate on the things we don't do well instead of patting ourselves on the back for all the good things we do. In the past, I have been intimidated by my own lack of education. Then I found out that, according to the Stanford Research Institute, success is 88 percent attitude and 12 percent education. That made sense to me, and it was just the inspiration I needed. What is your inspiration?

A prosperous lawyer friend of mine is successful as a sharp negotiator and investor in real estate. I asked him, as I have asked many other successful people, whether he thought being successful stems from education or from innate intelligence. "It definitely comes from inner smarts," he replied. The kind of smarts he meant are not necessarily intelligence, although the successful people he knows would not make stupid decisions or take foolish risks. "They just act on things a lot faster than the average person," he added. "They can weigh things and make up their minds more quickly. They know they *can* do it, they believe they *can* do it, and they *do* do it." So inner drive and inner talent, and especially a belief in oneself, are what seem to count for so much.

Bombing in Front of an Audience

Boo Bue, an international management trainer and a Dale Carnegie sponsor for Hawaii, told me how he first became acquainted with that marvelous organization: "I used to do some speaking for Remington Rand, about a ten- or fifteen-minute memorized talk that went with a film on office procedure. One day in July of 1950—I'll never forget it—at the University of Hawaii, they had to block off the windows to make it dark. The buildings were not air-conditioned in Hawaii in those days, so it got warm and uncomfortable. And then the picture was not synchronized with the sound. It was a mess.

"By this time, I really became nervous. Then I got up to speak, and the chairman—I couldn't believe it—put a piece of paper in my hands and said, 'Would you please cover these three points.'

"Well, it should have been easy but it wasn't my memorized talk. Have you ever been really embarrassed in front of a group? A physical change came over me. In the Dale Carnegie courses that I was later to teach, I could really empathize with people because of that experience. My stomach was churning. I knew my heart was going through my coat. My voice was up about three octaves. It was terrible.

"The next day I was in downtown Honolulu in a coffee shop. In those days, Honolulu was a very small community. You saw everybody you knew downtown. I ran into a person I knew had been in the audience the day before. I thought I would go up to her and say, 'Well, I didn't do so well,' and she'd say, 'Oh, you were all right. People always do that.' So, I walked up to her and I said, 'I didn't do so well,' and she said, 'You were awful.' My heart dropped. She was a nice person, not one you would think would be so blunt. Then she said, 'You ought to attend Dale Carnegie.' That was my turning point.

"The first year after taking the course, I doubled my income. The course increased my confidence that much." Needless to say, my friend Boo never found himself in a similarly distressing situation.

Those of us in business must stay on our toes. Whenever we get the feeling that everything is great, it's time to take a look around. As Max Gunther says in *The Luck Factor*, "Never, never, never assume you are fortune's darling. Lucky people are those who adapt to an environment of uncertainty. . . . I don't believe that in business or in life you can ever just coast."

Judging by Appearance

Early in my hairstyling career, a computer programmer for a major clothing company came to my salon. He was a pleasant man, a little overweight, plainly but nicely dressed. His hair was greased down. I shampooed and conditioned his hair, then totally restyled it. He went back to his office, where the women remarked on how good he looked. He went home and his wife thought he looked terrific. In just a few days, he realized he was looking pretty nifty! He was inspired to lose about twenty-five pounds, buy some fashionable new clothes, and start acting in a more outgoing manner. His bosses noticed this change and offered him a sales job, even though he had no sales experience. In a very short time, he was so successful that his territory was split five times, his income almost tripled and he began enjoying his work in a way he had never dreamed possible.

Am I saying this happened all because of a haircut? No. But his changed appearance changed his feelings about himself. He was inspired to act more confidently, and new opportunities opened up.

Because I realized I could influence people's lives in a positive way, I jumped out of bed with more enthusiasm each morning. It has been said that I offered "spiritual uplifting" along with the haircuts I gave. Perhaps, perhaps not—but I discovered that people were more likely to return to my salon if they felt better as well as looked better.

A New Image

George Sardonis was an engineer for a large company when I first met him at a Dale Carnegie class. He realized that the only way to earn more money was to go into sales. So he became an accounts receivable consultant for a major credit company. He was very determined. He went right out and knocked on thirty doors, but nobody would talk to him. He came to my salon and said, "Help! What can you do?"

George was an athletic, muscular man, with an overabundance of hair, a mustache and sideburns. In a business suit, he didn't fit the professional image of the time. I cut off a lot of his hair, removed his sideburns, and shaved his mustache. He went out again with the same presentation. This time he was accepted. After he had been a salesman for only four months, he was 280 percent above quota.

George went on to be one of the best salespeople in the country. Did he achieve this because of his appearance? Not totally. But by not offending people with his appearance, he obviously got there a lot faster. His appearance certainly contributed to his success.

Again, I'm not saying that he became a top salesperson just because of his appearance. But how he appeared to others made him think about himself differently. In Dale Carnegie courses, they teach that outer appearance reflects one's self-image. When people feel they look better, they feel more positive about themselves, and they can often achieve much better results.

A $1000 Investment

In 1975 communications expert Joan Minninger decided to expand the successful seminars she had been doing for the Civil Service

Commission into training programs for major corporations. She made two investments totaling $1,000—a lot of money at the time and a major sacrifice for Joan, who was existing month-to-month after a divorce. "I went to one of the best stores in town and spent $500 for one designer outfit with two silk blouses. That was my uniform. In 1975 $500 was a lot of money for an outfit, but I decided I was going to hit the corporate world. The other big expenditure was $500 for watermarked stationery. I learned later that my first big contract at General Electric was partly due to that stationery. The training manager liked my presentation, but the clincher was the fancy paper. In fact, my future husband confessed later that the reason we met, the only reason he attended one of my seminars, was that the training manager was so enthusiastic about the paper: 'She must be dynamite. Look at that watermarked stationery!'"

Of course Joan had the talent to follow through—her book *Total Recall: How to Boost Your Memory Power* has sold over 100,000 copies, and she works for a dozen major corporations—but it was the initial "package" that got her in the door.

Bad Times, Good Haircuts

In 1974, when there was a recession in America (although the hairstyling business escaped it), I was invited to go on a radio talk show in San Francisco, two hours in prime time. The exposure was very good for me professionally. Before we went on the air, the interviewer, Art Finley, revealed that his wife cut his hair. He said, "Patricia, I want you to tell wives how to cut their husbands' hair so they can economize during the recession." I told Mr. Finley that I thought he had an absolute nerve to invite a hairstylist to tell wives how to cut their husbands' hair. Then I said, "What I will do is go on the air and tell everybody why, when times are hard and you perhaps need more money, you should invest in a good haircut." When I got on the air, I did just that.

Why is it so important for us to look good? When times are difficult, I do not want to buy anything—a car, insurance, or even a washing machine—from somebody who looks as if he or she isn't making a good living at it. I don't want to think that I am the first—or last—customer. I always encourage young salespeople, even if they don't have much money, to invest in a good haircut, even if they have to wait an extra couple of weeks between visits to the styling shop. If they can only afford one good suit, they should press it every night. They should always *look* successful. They will feel better about themselves. They will project a much better image to their customers. And they will get better results.

What Your Hands Say

One of my customers from my salon days, Al Stanton, told me about a friend named Lyle Guslander. They went to Alameda High School together. After they graduated, Lyle Guslander went to Cornell University and studied hotel administration. After college he became the assistant manager of a large hotel in San Francisco.

One day, walking along Market Street in San Francisco, Al Stanton met Lyle, who invited him to look around the hotel. Lyle was animated and talked a lot with his hands. After Al had been escorted all over, he said to Lyle, "Do you mind if I give you some friendly criticism? Your fingernails are absolutely terrible. They are broken, uneven, and dirty. You speak so much with your hands — you're almost constantly showing brochures and price lists to people — it really gives a bad first impression."

Lyle never forgot that advice. He eventually went to Hawaii, where he owned many hotels, including the Royal Lahaina Resort. Later, he sold the chain to the AMFAC corporation, where he became a senior vice president with that company.

Several years later, Al Stanton was in Hawaii and went to see his old friend, who called his staff into the office and said, "This is the gentleman who made me aware of how much appearance and grooming can improve your chance for success. He made me aware that I had to change my poorly manicured hands."

Now, maybe Lyle Guslander would have become very successful anyway. But by not turning people off along the way with dirty fingernails, he obviously furthered his career.

When Opportunity Knocks, Be Dressed for It

One of Britain's most beloved performers for three decades, Gracie Fields, told of an incident that changed forever how she presented herself in public. It was one of those gloomy, slushy, depressing midwinter days that Britain is noted for, and "Our Gracie" decided to attend a matinee performance of a musical in which a friend was appearing. With clunky galoshes, an old raincoat, and her hair in strings from the sleet outside, she made her way to her seat. To her chagrin, her friend stepped to the footlights and called Gracie up on stage to take a bow. "There I was, galoshes flopping, a thoroughly rumpled raincoat, no makeup, and my hair plastered to my head. All these people were applauding a 'star' and I looked like a derelict. I learned then never to leave the house unless I looked my best."

Before speaking at a morning program for women at an exclusive department store in the San Francisco area, I was wandering through the audience, as is my habit, introducing myself to the people in attendance. Out of the corner of my eye I noticed one of the most stunning women I'd ever seen. She wore a simple but well-coordinated outfit, a blouse, skirt, and hat. (I wondered why I never looked like that in a blouse and skirt!)

It was obvious from the way she carried and conducted herself that she must be someone successful. I was so attracted by her smile and general appearance that I walked over, thrust out my hand and said, "I know you must be somebody important, and I'd like to meet you." I was greeting Diane Parente, who turned out to be as friendly as she was attractive.

She had been in fashion for fourteen years and was then a wardrobe consultant. I told her she should be giving workshops and introduced her to the store manager. He booked her to speak at one of the store's programs a month or so later. (Like newspaper columnist Doug Hooper, she said 'yes' immediately, even though she had never given talks before. If she had thought about it, she might well have said 'no', blocking a whole new area for her career.) Since that day, I have used her services and have recommended her to dozens of other people, as well as becoming one of her best friends. This is a perfect example of how looking successful helps you sell your services.

The Odds for Failure

If you expect failure, the odds are overwhelming that you will fail. Having confidence that you will succeed improves the probability of success. To achieve success, then, a person must develop self-confidence, learn not to fear risk. The only way to do that is *actually* to try something that results in the feeling of success.

Many of us are unsuccessful and unadventurous because we tried something once, didn't do it well, and have never tried again. I can remember several years ago when I started demonstrating haircutting. The audiences were so unimpressed, I pitied myself. But by getting up time and time again, I slowly became one of the top hairstyling demonstrators in the country. Whenever I stood up to try again, I concentrated on how good I was going to be in the future instead of reliving the unsuccessful past attempts. Time and practice improve us.

Charging What You're Worth

Jack Peterson, the photographer, says, "You also have to believe in what you yourself can do. People ask me why I charge so much to give a speech. What I charge reflects what I feel I am worth. In my lectures, I ask photographers what they charge for an 8" x 10" photo. Person A will say $8.95, person B will say $9.95, and so on. Then I ask how they arrived at the price. 'Well,' the answer goes, 'it costs so much for the film and so much for the paper, times three, and that's what I come up with.' Then I tell them they're missing the whole point. What are *you* worth as an individual? What did it take for you to get where you are today? How much studying did you have to do? How much inborn talent and insight do you possess? That's what you base your fee on, because this is what the customer is paying for.

"The paper costs all of us the same amount of money. The difference is the talent that puts the image on the paper. That's what you charge for. When you start thinking that way, you'll become a better photographer — and you will become a better person."

Who Would You Rather Be?

Being a better person . . . isn't this, after all, what it's all about — to make ourselves better people? Earl Nightingale suggests that when we are feeling a little disturbed about our jobs or our lives, we should ask ourselves these questions:

☆ Is there anyone else on earth I would like to be?

☆ Is there any other place I would like to be?

☆ Is there any other career I would like to pursue?

☆ If I could do it again, would I go back to being twelve?

When we are disenchanted, we should question ourselves and realize we are capable of changing things more than we give ourselves credit for.

Boosting a Poor Self-Image

In *Fear of Success*, Leon Tec says, "In spite of their accomplishments, there often appear people who fear success because they have a poor self-image, an image they do not like."

Similarly, many women come to me in my seminars and say, "I tell my husband he's wonderful and I give him positive strokes, but his father told him he would never amount to anything." Such an individual has a poor self-image. Poor self-images are tough to deal with. But even if your spouse doesn't respond to praise, you should still give it — if you believe it. Just say, "You did that so well" or "I really appreciate your patience."

We need to understand those who suffer — and suffer they do — from low self-esteem. One woman told me that her husband says she's crazy whenever she compliments him.

"Obviously, he has low self-esteem," I said.

And she said, "Well, yes, probably because he cannot read or write."

"Have you asked him to learn? Have you encouraged him?" I asked.

"Yes, but he's bothered by it and I guess he doesn't like to admit that he can't. So instead of dealing with it, he ignores it."

I asked whether he had a boss who could support him in confronting the problem. She said, "No, he's self-employed as a bricklayer."

This woman goes to church but her husband doesn't, so she could not get the minister to talk to him. I said, "Well, the best thing I can suggest is to keep telling him he's wonderful. Maybe you're the only person telling him, but it's important that he get some boosting from someone."

When someone can't accept compliments because of poor self-esteem, you have to shift recognition to the person's activities or actions. Say, "I really appreciate that." Performance that is rewarded tends to be repeated. In *The One Minute Manager*, Ken Blanchard recommends catching people when they do something right and complimenting them. He says, "We have to make deposits in people's emotional bank accounts."

Too Late for Self-Esteem?

Self-esteem, of course, starts quite early. Many people at seminars tell me it's too late for them — utter nonsense, of course — but they wish their kids could hear what I have to say. Even if you have bought the fable that it's too late for you, it is important to start influencing your children positively.

My friend Jeanne Robertson, one of the top humorous speakers in the country, says that when she was thirteen, she was six-feet-two-inches tall with size eleven feet. She is sure her parents used to close their door at night and say, "Oh, my God, she's still growing." But her parents never let her think anything was wrong, Jeanne says. "You think children are cruel, but when I was thirteen, walking down the street trying to get my arms and legs going in the same direction, grown men would come up and look up at me and say, 'Hey, little girl, how tall are you?'"

When she visited her relatives, they would say, "Oh my, how you've grown." Jeanne's parents helped her with comic retorts. She would jump out of the car and say, "Oh my, how I've grown." So her parents developed not only her sense of humor but her self-esteem — two things all of us can use in abundance. Jeanne is famous for showing people how to laugh at the things they can't change.

Never Assume

A rule for scientific researchers is "never assume." None of us are mind readers, but we often assume people know what we think when they really don't. People know only how we act. Psychologist Luann Lindquist says one of the big problems in communicating is that we assume too much — and when you split up the word "assume," she contends, it makes an "ass" out of "u" and "me." We *assume* that what works for us works for everyone else, but that isn't necessarily true. We each need our strokes, but often in different ways.

Getting a Boost

Getting a boost, a positive affirmation, when you are in the middle of a growing experience can make all the difference. Sometimes the affirmation may come at just the right moment — and from an unexpected source.

When my friend Bob Jansen was twenty-three years old (quite a few years ago), he was in show business. One night he was going to sing in a beautiful Chicago auditorium, one of the largest in the area. As he was getting dressed, making up his face, and trying to make himself as handsome as possible, an old-timer came in and asked, "Are you nervous, kid?"

"Yes, I certainly am," Bob replied.

And the old-timer said, "Well, let me tell you something: When you go out there on that stage, you have to realize you are the best singer in this auditorium. If there were a singer in this auditorium better than you, he or she would be up there—not you." Jansen claims that that was the confidence booster he needed at just that moment.

YOUR ASSIGNMENT:
What Am I Telling Others?

*Andrew Lloyd Weber: Tell me,
Stephen — you're so popular. Why is it that
people dislike me the minute they meet me?*

Stephen Sondheim: . . . saves time.

Imaginary conversation
reported by columnist Liz Smith

	Yes	No
1. Do I dress neatly and appropriately for each business occasion?	[ ]	[ ]
2. Is my eye communication good and steady?	[ ]	[ ]
3. Is my posture comfortable and self-confident?	[ ]	[ ]
4. Do I sit erect?	[ ]	[ ]
5. Are my gestures natural?	[ ]	[ ]
6. Do I give the appearance of being self-confident (even when I'm not)?	[ ]	[ ]
7. Is my voice natural and my conversation spontaneous?	[ ]	[ ]

	Yes	No
8. Do I have any nervous mannerisms and do I use any irritating non-words ("ur's," "ah's")?	[ ]	[ ]
9. Am I a good listener?	[ ]	[ ]
10. Have I ever listened to a recording of myself in an important situation? (If not, why not?)	[ ]	[ ]
11. If I met somebody important in the supermarket at 9:00 A.M. on a Saturday, would I feel I had to apologize for my appearance?	[ ]	[ ]
12. Do I take a sincere interest in other people when I first meet them?	[ ]	[ ]
13. If the answer to any of the above questions is "No," what am I going to do about it?	[ ]	[ ]

CHAPTER 9

Personal Communication

"What you are speaks so loudly, I cannot hear what you say."

Ralph Waldo Emerson

When I arrived at a major San Francisco company to present a time management seminar, I found a crew of already-well-organized secretaries. What they needed to learn was how to manage their managers.

My first assignment was for them to make a priority list of their job activities, what they considered the ten most important things they did. Their second assignment was to get their supervisors to make a similar list—how the supervisor rated the priority of the secretary's tasks. When I returned a week later, we compared the lists.

You may not be surprised that, in this Fortune 500 company, one with a stellar reputation for organization, some secretaries not only had listed their duties in an entirely different order of priority than their bosses had, but often they and their bosses had listed entirely different activities.

Before you can manage time, you need to know what you are supposed to be doing with it. When you work for someone else, this means that performance appraisal is essential, whether it is formal or informal. If you give me a list of ten things to do and I do only five, you may wonder why I did the least important five. Success depends on communicating priorities.

When Employees Talk to the Boss

In business today, straightforward communication is imperative. This means from the top down and from the bottom up. I always ask executives one question: When was the last time you asked your assistant, your secretary, or anyone working under you what you could do to make his or her job easier?

Top managers who complain about poorly motivated employees should hear what I hear from the people under them. These administrative assistants and managers complain to me, "We're all revved up. We're going to get organized—but our boss is so disorganized."

"Why don't you go to your boss," I tell them, "and say, 'I would like to earn the money you pay me by doing more than I do now. Perhaps if you gave me your priority projects before you left at night, when I arrive in the morning—in that hour of peace and quiet before you arrive—I can do those important things.'"

Do you know how many people reply that they couldn't possibly say that to their boss? A *successful* workplace has an environment in which people feel free to submit new ideas.

Boo Bue once told me about a superintendent of a large mill that had a two-part problem with its production line: It couldn't keep the lines coordinated, and it had too many rejects. Management had never quite been able to solve these problems. Using the creative thinking concept he had learned at Dale Carnegie seminars, the superintendent got his workers together and said, "I need your help. We've got this production line that just isn't staying coordinated and causes too many rejects. We need your thinking. What can we do to solve the problems?"

After a while, an older man came to the superintendent and said, "I've got an idea I think would work." They tried it. In no time at all, the lines became coordinated, the rejects were reduced, and the company saved a thousand dollars a day.

They had a recognition dinner for the employee. As the boss was patting him on the back, the guy confessed that he'd had the idea for five years. Stunned, the boss said, "Five years! Why haven't you told us?" "You never asked me," the man replied. Now they have a suggestion box—a great big one.

Getting Them on Your Side

But a suggestion box — even a large one — won't solve all your communication problems. It's a foolish manager who implements every suggestion offered by an employee. It's an equally foolish manager who constantly ignores suggestions.

One manager who really knew how to involve his employees was Richard Calton. Twenty-five years ago he lived in Southern California, where he successfully managed people in a grocery distribution business. A man from Northern California asked Calton to work for him because, the man explained, he had a morale problem in a similar business. The company had also lost $2 million the previous year.

When young Calton went to work for the company, he found that his work force included seven men who had just been released — perhaps too soon — from San Quentin Prison through a rehabilitation hiring program. On Calton's first day on the job, an employee refused to speak to him: "Don't talk to me, talk to my shop steward." Within the first week, Calton's car was stolen. (Admittedly this was less dramatic than what happened to the car of the man who hired him: *His* car had been torched.) A suggestion box stuffed with cigarette butts typified worker- management communication.

The first thing the new young manager undoubtedly did was wonder why he had ever left Southern California. The next thing, however, was to realize the need for immediate communication as part of a much larger program to restore strict discipline. He began by asking the men their opinion on certain matters — fairly simple things to start: What sort of yarn — thick, medium, or thin — should be used to tie the boxes with? What color lines should be painted on the floor, red, blue, or yellow?

An interesting thing happened. For the first time the workers became involved in the company. It was the first time they had been asked what *they* thought.

Then another interesting thing happened: Production increased. Suddenly everyone's enthusiasm became aroused. Calton began to involve the workers in more important decisions. He asked for feedback on the type of equipment the company should be using. The real turning point occurred when he purchased two expensive pieces of equipment that the workers claimed didn't work. Calton spied his opportunity and asked them to recommend equipment to replace equipment that would work. On their own time, two men drove from

San Francisco to Southern California, 450 miles each way, to look at equipment. Calton bought what they recommended. As a group, they made history in the grocery distribution business.

Calton realized that many of his employees' ideas would not work. But rather than say, "That's a dumb idea," he said, "Let's try it." Even using less efficient techniques, production increased because the men *wanted* their ideas to work. When a technique wasn't working, they would say, "Hey, boss, let's go back to the old way." Some things, such as delivering at night, went against their union contract, but since the men were part of the decision-making process, they helped renegotiate the contract.

Well, it was very pleasant that everyone was happy and fulfilled, but some people will want to know the bottom line. At the end of the first year, the company had lost $20,000. The next year, it made $150,000 profit. In three years, it made $500,000 profit. At the end of five years, the company was earning $750,000 a year and had paid off the $2 million debt.

Calton had thought of many of the employees' suggestions independently, but he shared the glory and encouraged them. He did not say, "Oh, I thought about that," or "Well, I tried that before and it didn't work." Instead, he encouraged them to think for themselves and feel a part of what was happening. Many managers, in order to justify their position or their salary, think they have to come up with all the ideas and solve all the problems. What a good manager does, what Richard Calton did, is create an environment where people are encouraged to think and participate.

Even when things were running smoothly, Calton would create a problem. "Okay, guys, I've got a problem. I need your help." He did this to give his employees something to think about and to work on. Years later I met some of the men who worked for Calton at that time. Two of them considered him the best boss they had ever had. One of them was driving garbage trucks at Lake Tahoe and owned a small motel with his wife. Whenever problems arose, he would say, "We should have Calton here. He would straighten this out."

Unspoken Agreements

We have to make sure that people can talk to us. When people feel they can't, they are going to complain to others. That wastes time, energy, and creates a climate in which it is difficult for anyone to go forward. Complainers may feel better temporarily, but they have done nothing toward solving the problem. The person who "caused" the complaint gains nothing except a sense that something is wrong. Even the innocent listener loses — he or she feels helpless, frustrated, and goes away suspecting that the problems of the XYZ Corporation are insoluble.

We need to get the unspoken agreements out of the closet. For example, a group of insurance workers in San Francisco took a time management seminar. Outside their usual workplace, they were able to discuss things they had never talked about before. They realized two of the biggest problems back at the office were unnecessary socializing and unnecessary interruptions, so they came up with a system. They made a batch of small paper flags. When someone put a paper flag on his or her desk, it meant, "Do not interrupt me unless the building is burning down." They solved what they considered a major problem with a simple solution.

The insignificant things that are not communicated build up. Many people have quit companies where they could have had wonderful careers because they never discussed the seemingly silly, insignificant things with others. When people leave, they take the problems with them — and often have the same problems in the next place.

Recognizing Great Ideas

In *No More Beans: The Restaurant That Won the West*, historian Carla Kelly tells us that travelers in the early days of the transcontinental railroad had more to fear from the food served at the restaurants along the way than from Indian raids, desperadoes, and burned-out axle bearings.

An obscure employee of the Chicago, Burlington and Quincy Railroad approached his superiors with the idea that the railroad and restaurants ought to work together to offer edible, reasonably priced food. This immigrant-employee proposed that the railroads provide the rooms for the restaurant, plus free freighting of food and transportation for employees, and free ice, coal and water. The cafe owner would supply the equipment for the buildings and provide the workers and the food; train crews would be allowed to eat at half-price. He reasoned that if the food and the service were good enough, the restaurant might even make money and the railroad would satisfy the customers and its own crews. Well-fed travelers were more likely to frequent the same route if they knew they could get a well-cooked meal that would not land them in the hospital.

The Chicago, Burlington and Quincy did not act on the idea. The Atchison, Topeka and Santa Fe Railroad did, however, and "for nearly fifteen years, a handshake was the only contract needed to implement one of the southwest's miracles — meals by Fred Harvey." Harvey meals, Harvey Houses and Harvey girls have remained something of a legend — right down to the Hollywood movie *The Harvey Girls* starring Judy Garland.

Enthusiasm in the Ranks

Five years ago I spoke in Cleveland for Ohio Bell. The driver who met me at the airport was a walking press agent for the company. He'd been with them twenty-three years. At the offices, two secretaries matched his enthusiasm. One of them said, "The way our company is going, in two years [after divestiture], there probably won't be a job for us. But the experience of working for these people is so exciting we don't care if we lose our jobs." You can always tell what a company is like by talking to the people on the lower rungs.

When I met their boss, Jim Croll, I asked what he did to establish such loyalty in the company, something that is a lot more difficult to do in a big company than in a small company. He told me that every couple of months he sat down with his employees to have a "three-on-three" session. "I say, 'In managing you, what three things do I do that you like, that I should do more of? And what three things do I do that you don't like, that I should do less of?'"

Jim Croll was opening himself up for *feedback*, not criticism. Insecure managers often see any negative comments as a threat, an attempt to undermine their authority. But when managers can do this, they set the stage for their employees to say, "Here's what you're doing right, and here's what needs improvement. Can I do anything to help you?"

Your Source of Power

As Michael Korda states in his book *Power*, there are two types of power: personal power and position power. The position power says you're the general, you're the boss, you're the CEO, the teacher, the parent, the guard in charge of this cell block. You hold power only as long as you hold the position.

But with personal power, people *want* to help you accomplish your goals. The power goes with you wherever you go because it is part of you. Think of the politicians, businessmen, and generals who fade from sight as soon as they lose their titles, while others remain imposing leaders and venerable "elder statesmen" without any official status. (Former presidents provide a good sampling of both.)

Three Good Management Musts

Delegating. Good management means delegating and always rewarding a job well done. Managers sometimes feel that they can do things better and faster — which is often true. But unless you take the time to train people to help you, you'll look around for help in a real emergency and discover that everyone lacks experience. Teach your employees what you want and expect them to do. Then to be sure they understand your instructions, ask them to tell you what they think they've heard. (Avoid "upward delegation." When employees bring you problems to solve, tell them to go away and return with three possible solutions.)

Training. Don't invest more time in training people than they are willing to give you. It is a fact of life that some people are more ambitious than others. We often are disappointed when people don't live up to our expectations. Look at the people around you and notice who is eager to grow and develop, and who isn't. Avoid disappointment. Be more realistic.

Rewarding. Learn to reward people with something other than money, such as recognition and education. As long as people are getting benefits from helping you, they will do things for free. When I was training hairstylists, I found that many people would give me extra assistance without pay. They were happy to help out for the extra training.

The Poodle Comes First

Arvella Schuller was one of five speakers at a rally I addressed in San Diego. She is the wife of Dr. Robert Schuller, minister of Garden Grove. Arvella produces her husband's television show, and has both a career and a family.

She once asked a psychologist whether there were many different marriage problems or the same problem occurring over and over. The psychologist said, "Basically, all the marriage problems I see could be summed up in two words: one is *selfishness* and the second is *immaturity*." He recalled one woman saying, "I would like to be treated by my husband the way he treats the poodle. When he comes home, he talks to the poodle and he touches the poodle." When the psychologist told this to the husband, he said, "Well, I wish that my wife would act like the poodle. When I come home, the poodle is obviously pleased to see me."

What Does "Communication" Mean to You?

In *The Magic of Rapport*, authors Jerry Richardson and Joel Margulis point out that communication means different things to different people. Couples often go into counseling because of "communication problems" arising from different ideas of what communication means. In a typical first interview, the counselor might turn to the wife and ask her what the problem is. Many wives reply, "He just never listens to anything I say." To the husband, the problem might be, "She doesn't look at me when I'm talking to her." Or, either might think the other unfeeling and uncaring because he or she is "not very affectionate" or "emotionally responsive."

When each partner is trying to communicate in a different mode, the counselor tries to make them aware of what's going on, of how each is asking something alien of the other. The next step might be to get each person to learn to communicate in ways that are meaningful to the other. In the case above, for example, the counselor might encourage the husband to pay more attention to what the wife is saying. The wife might be advised to establish eye contact with her husband more frequently to "show" him that she's paying attention to him.

The Saddest Thing

What is more important in our lives than communication? One of the saddest things I've heard from behind the barber's chair was confided by a fellow Englishman in his late forties: "I went to England just to tell my father that I loved him. I don't think I've done it before."

It is sad when people don't share feelings, when they've been brought up to be unemotional. The good feelings you have for others mean absolutely nothing unless they know how you feel.

Husbands' Secrets

An article written in the 1970s claimed I was the best authority on marriage because of my years behind the styling chair talking to men all day long about their relationships. One woman called me and asked, "If I buy a gift certificate for my husband and send him to you for his haircut, will you find out what he thinks about our marriage? Then I'll meet you afterwards and you can tell me." The fact that people often reveal intimate things to their hairstylists does not offset how sad it is that the woman couldn't ask her own husband what he thought of their marriage.

Hiding from Delight

If we take the time to sit and chat with people, we can learn a good many things about life — even from our spouses! I learned this quite early. There was a woman who used to frequent the hairdressing salon in England where I first apprenticed. I was fifteen years old. She was a rather large, unattractive woman with gray hair. I would always slip away and pretend to be busy when she appeared at the shop. One time, however, I didn't hide quickly enough. During the twenty minutes I had to make conversation with her, I realized what a totally fascinating woman she was — something I would never have known had I continued to avoid her. I was lucky indeed for having been forced to get in touch with her. It was a lesson I have never forgotten.

Seven Minutes to Say "Thank You"

Staying in touch is as important as getting in touch. Long-time sales trainer Bill Gove used to be sales manager for the 3M Company, and he used to write a lot of thank- you notes. One day someone was teasing him and said, "Hey, Bill, all you do is write notes all day long."

He said, "No, seven minutes a day. Everybody that does business with me hears from me at least once every three months, while my competition is calling on them asking for their business."

As a result of hearing his story, I used to write to my hairstyling customers as I do to my speaking clients today, thanking them for the opportunity to serve them. One of my customers, Hank Torchiani, used to come in at 7:45 in the morning once a month for the last eight years that I had my salon. One day I dropped him this note: "Hank, have I told you recently how much I love waking up with you once a month?" (Naturally I sent that to his office, not his home. I'm not a trouble maker!) But the next time he came in he said, "Patricia, that was such a nice note, I'm keeping it in my box of treasures." He died in 1987 and I am very grateful I had communicated how much I enjoyed not only his patronage but also his friendship.

What a Personal Note Can Do

My friend Boo tells about his neighbor, George Dashiell, who was brought in as Vice President of Sales for Memorex to help save it from going down the tubes. After the turn-around was successful, George moved down to Newport Beach to head up another company. George believed in recognizing people. To get his staff stirred up, he once wrote about a hundred personal letters to the people who had worked overtime. Here is a typical letter.

Dear Dave:

The manager has told me that you worked extra hours during the holiday season. I want you to know how much all of us appreciate this. We hope it was not too inconvenient for you or your family, especially around Christmas.

Your willingness to make this special effort to help us reach a new shipment record was not only an expression of job efficiency, but it displays an attitude on which great companies are built.

Our very best wishes to you and your family for a healthy, happy, and successful new year.

Dashiell got a reaction he had never seen before. He had husbands and wives of his employees calling him on the phone to tell him that their spouses had been working for years, and this was the first time they had ever received a letter telling them they were appreciated. Dashiell said he could feel the excitement and the electricity.

The letters were sent to the employees' homes so their families would see them. This way their families shared the enjoyment, for they, after all, were being thanked as well.

Letters of appreciation *have* to be genuine. They can't be "formula" public relations pieces. Employees and customers spot phony, self-serving sentiments immediately and resent them even more than they resent being ignored. These anecdotes are not intended to get you to turn out bulk mailings, just to emphasize the tremendous value of expressing your real gratitude.

A writer friend, Eleanor Dugan, told me about some unusual thank you letters she once sent. "When a popular newscaster died, I suddenly realized how many public figures there are who become an important and positive part of our lives, but we never bother to thank them. Then they're gone. So I sat down and sent notes to about a dozen people, mostly old-time performers who were no longer in the limelight, school teachers who had helped me, salespeople, librarians. If I didn't know how to reach them, I addressed them in care of organizations they probably belonged to like SAG (Screen Actors Guild) or found their names in their hometown phone books if they had retired. The amazing thing is that over the course of the next year, every one of those people, even the famous ones, replied with delightful and moving letters. I found out later that one of the people received my letter the day that he was fired from a job he had held for many years. I like to think that my letter helped get him through that day, because his response was warm and upbeat."

Letters to Cry Over

Bill Coors, head of Coors Brewery in Denver, decided to write letters to everybody in the company. He wrote to his secretary, who had also worked for his father before him. After she got the letter telling her what a great job she was doing, she went to the front office and closed the door. She had tears in her eyes, and said, "You know, I really love my job and I'm very well taken care of by the company. But this is the first time in all the years I've worked for Coors that anybody really has said, 'I appreciate what you're doing.'"

A lot of times we just take for granted that others know how we feel, but more often than not they don't. Not only do letters of genuine recognition work in business, they work in personal life. I frequently write notes to my friends telling them how much I appreciate their friendship, and they write to me. It's one thing to say it—it's another to take the time and trouble to write it. And very often you can say things in a letter you wouldn't say in person, because, face-to-face, you may feel a bit shy.

Having a successful life isn't just accomplishing great goals or having big exciting things happen. It also means paying attention to the little things—like thank-you notes—that can make such a difference in our daily life.

YOUR ASSIGNMENT:
Unspoken Agreements

Have I gotten into "unspoken agreements" with people that I would like to clarify and maybe change?

What things should I clearly and rationally discuss with:

My spouse?

My children?

My parents?

My brothers/sisters?

My workmates?

My boss?

My best friends?

Other people I come in contact with regularly?

Who should I write to today?

CHAPTER 10

Associating With People

"Our life is frittered away by detail."

Henry David Thoreau

The English romantic poet William Wordsworth wrote that "the world is too much with us," that "getting and spending, we lay waste our power." If this was true in the nineteenth century (and who doubts it?), things have surely gotten worse. How much time and emotional energy do you spend frivolously, in pursuit of you know not what or doing something with someone—anyone—just so you feel you're getting somewhere?

As a single person I am amazed how many of my attractive, intelligent, single friends, male and female, prefer a date with *anybody* rather than staying home alone. Illustrating this dilemma is a cartoon from *New Woman* magazine. A woman writes in her diary, "Dear diary, I don't normally sleep with a man on the first date; however, Fred was an exception; he was so boring I dozed off during dinner!"

Three Kinds of People to Get Rid Of

To become the person you are capable of being, you have to grow away from the people, habits, and thoughts that keep you from the life you want to lead. We'll talk about the habits and thoughts later. Let's start with the people. The people who don't belong in your life fall into three categories.

1. People who are consistently unsupportive

2. People with whom you have nothing in common

3. People who are negative and depressing

1. The Non-Supporters

People who don't support you, who even make a practice of shooting you down in the name of "honesty," should be the first to go. First imagine a great victory. Perhaps you got a promotion, perhaps you lost twenty pounds, perhaps you ran five miles for the first time — imagine whatever a great win for you would be. Now imagine telling your spouse, your boss, your best friend, or your mother-in-law about your achievement. What do you think his or her automatic response would be? Would it be, "Hey, terrific, you can do it again"? Or "Hey, that's a fluke"? Or even an incredulous,"You?!"? If you are deliberately surrounding yourself with people who delight in shooting you down, getting the life you want will be much, much harder.

Of course, not everyone who fails to support us has evil intentions, either consciously or unconsciously. And criticism can be a powerful catalyst. Most of us can remember someone who, justly or unjustly, chewed our tails and made us reassess ourselves. Often this is a major turning point in our lives.

But one of the reasons we sometimes don't develop ourselves fully is that we choose to surround ourselves with people who tell us we can't do things. Even people who love us commit this error with the best of intentions. They don't want to see us hurt, they don't want to see us disappointed, or they are trying to protect us. (This happens a lot, I'm sure, in marriages and with parents.)

When I was thirty years old and had a well-paying job, my father told me not to go into business for myself. "Your staff," he warned, "will drive you crazy."

I said, "Father, I know my staff will drive me crazy. But you were in business for yourself when you were thirty. I'm thirty. I've got to do it."

My father hadn't spent any real time with me since I left home at eighteen. I was living on another continent. Although I went home on vacation and talked to my parents regularly, my father didn't know who I had become and what my capabilities were. The best thing for my relationship with my father was his coming to America and seeing me in my own environment. In our parents' minds, we never grow up, even when the roles reverse and we take care of them.

When you start planning what you want out of life, it is very important to discuss your plans with peers, mentors, and role models. But be aware that the people who are closest to you and have the best intentions may not necessarily give you the best advice. We want the ones we love to support us — but this may not always be easy for them to do.

Teachers play a strong role in shaping our self-image, for better or worse. Fortunately a teacher's lack of support can sometimes stimulate healthy rebellion, an "I'll show you" response. Paul Mitchell, a hairstylist of national prominence, wanted to be an actor. His mother, a hairdresser herself in Scotland, insisted he get his hairdresser's license first. Paul was tall, lanky, and rather clumsy. The owner of the hairstyling school told him he was too awkward ever to make it as a hairdresser. Just to develop his confidence for the stage, Paul began entering hairstyling contests. To his surprise, he won most of them. Paul became famous as one of Vidal Sassoon's stars. He left to open his own school in New York and now he lives in Hawaii. His hair products company, Paul Mitchell Professional Hair Care Products, is probably the fastest- growing one in the United States. Once Paul became famous, the owner of the school wanted to advertise that Paul was a former pupil. I'm sure Paul got great satisfaction out of saying, "No way."

Trish Britt echoes my cautionary note: "Don't be discouraged by people around you. I think your friends have to be really positive people, productive people, people who are encouraging you, who know you, and who reinforce you. It's easy just to sit around and say, 'Oh, that will never work,' and 'You won't try hard enough.' If you have positive people saying, 'Hey, that's a great idea' and 'When do you start?' — that's what's important."

2. The Nothing-in-Common's

Some people get into what I call the going-to-dinner syndrome. You have dinner with John and Mary every fourth Friday; then you invite them back, though you really don't know why. You don't look forward to it. You don't enjoy yourself. You don't come away feeling expanded and elated, full of new ideas and insights as you do with other encounters. Every time you have dinner with John and Mary, you go home swearing you'll never do it again.

If you spend three and a half hours one night a week socializing with people you don't enjoy being with and don't learn anything from, you waste four and a half work weeks of your year. That alone can keep you groveling on your economic knees.

I have a good friend—a former good friend. We worked together about seventeen years ago and had a terrific time, going to garage sales and flea markets every weekend, plays and movies—we loved it, and loved our friendship. It was very difficult for us to give this up because we'd been such great buddies. Now, understand, I'll always bail him out of jail. I'll make sure he never starves to death. But I will not invest an evening every couple of weeks to see him. Why? Because we have nothing in common any more. This does not invalidate the fact that we had many great times together. It does not invalidate the fact that we really love each other. It just means we have nothing in common, nothing that makes it worth spending time together. When you find that your get-togethers with an old friend consist of nothing but reminiscences of happy times past, that there is no *present*, then you know that it is time to move on. Please do yourself a favor: Say goodbye to the friends and acquaintances that no longer belong in your life.

3. The Downers

The final person you must eliminate from your life is the negative, depressing one, the "victim" of the world. If you are going to adapt to changes in the future, you cannot surround yourself with victims. Often we enjoy saving them, but for the wrong reason: It makes *us* feel good. Of course, it's great to do good deeds for altruistic reasons, but when the rescued doesn't benefit, even resents the rescuer's efforts, and the rescuer loses ground too, then it is an everybody-loses situation.

Let's consider how people often start their day. They go to work, go into the staff room, and hang around the coffee pot. There they listen to others talking about the miserable things in their lives. Many people automatically respond, "You think that's bad? You should hear what happened to me!" They're competing for being in the worst possible situation. One-downmanship.

Starting your day this way has a devastating effect on the way you feel. It doesn't matter how energetic you are when you go to work if you get knocked down the minute you arrive. You're not going to have the energy to do your job. Make sure the people around you don't drag you down. Low self-esteem—yours or anyone else's—drains your time and energy.

My brother Robert Fripp, of rock band King Crimson fame, said in a press conference that it was the first band he'd been in where no one had a major drinking problem, drug problem, or woman problem. He said, "This is my fifteenth year as a professional—do you know what it's like for the very first time to work with people and not have to worry that their personal problems will prevent them from getting on stage? Can you imagine going into a [business] office not knowing whether the people there can function because of their personal habits?"

What we often do—and shouldn't—is surround ourselves with people we know are unreliable, who constantly prove themselves to be unreliable. Sometimes we need to be in the midst of losers so we can feel in control. Sometimes we get a secret kick out of feeling superior to our companions—"compared to him, I really look good." This may be a very comfortable way to live, but it stunts our personal growth.

This doesn't mean that you can't accept the human frailties of others. But until people have committed themselves to positive change, you shouldn't carry the load for them. Find other people. You owe it to yourself.

The People on Your Side

Power in life and business comes from three things: who you are, whom you are perceived to be, and who is on your side. You can't choose your family, and if you are happy with your relatives it's a cause for major celebration. However, you *do* pick your friends, and the world generally lumps you in the same category with them. This simplistic assumption may not be entirely true, but it is age-old—Aesop had a fable about being judged by the company you keep.

Identify Your Cronies

Friends are great, but what you really want in life are some cronies. A crony is one step up from a friend, someone totally reliable. If you make a date to meet a crony at 6:15 in the morning and it is pouring rain, your crony will still be there at 6:14. I can honestly tell you that my women friends in San Francisco—my cronies—and our extended cronies in other cities get as excited about each other's success as we do about our own. It's good to have a forum where you can be proud of your accomplishments and feel support. It's equally valuable to be able to talk about disappointments and disasters with equal comfort. That's what cronies are for.

Being a close friend or crony doesn't mean you have to be in continuous contact. Because we all have such busy lives, my cronies and I get together irregularly, usually to celebrate each other's birthdays or holiday seasons. In honor of each other, we all dress up and look absolutely spectacular. At our dinners, in each other's homes or in restaurants, we take turns describing what's happening in our lives. Everybody gets to hear. (Have you ever had the frustrating experience of going to a dinner party and talking only to the two people on either side of you?) At our get-togethers, all are complimented on their appearance, as well as their achievements. We all agree that each other's friendship is one of the most cherished things in our lives, and this knowledge helps us weather the storms that everyone goes through periodically.

YOUR ASSIGNMENT:
Friendship

It has been said that if the end of the world was coming in ten minutes, every phone booth in America would be filled. Why wait? Start making your phone list below:

1. Which friends make me feel better whenever I call them just to say hello?

2. Do I have the same effect on them?

   If not, why not?

   If so, what is it about me that my friends like?

3. If I had just met me, would I want to be my friend?

4. When was the last time I did something nice for somebody with no thought of a reward?

TO DO: Say something true to the next three people you meet that will make them feel genuinely good about themselves.

CHAPTER 11

First Impressions

"Meeting him was like opening a bottle of champagne."

Winston Churchill, on meeting
Franklin D. Roosevelt

How do you make people feel when they first meet you? For one moment, pretend you are like a slice of bread. Are you mass-produced, bland, tasteless, stale? Or are you hot out of the oven, loaded with flavor and nutrients? Some breads look alike, but the first bite usually tells us what we are getting.

I've always tried to add more vitamins and a bit of crunch to myself, especially in what I give to others. Both *San Francisco Magazine* and the *Daily Commercial News* wrote that executives who came to my hair salon got a spiritual uplift along with their haircuts. Although I wouldn't go that far, I did discover that helping people feel good as well as look good made them more likely to return.

The Crucial Four Minutes

In *Contact: The First Four Minutes*, author Leonard Zunin asks, "Why four minutes? It is not an arbitrary interval. Rather, it is the average time, demonstrated by careful observation, during which strangers in a social situation interact before they decide to part or continue their encounter." Zunin pleads with spouses to give the first four minutes to their mates when they come home from work. Don't talk about problems until a pleasant mood has been established.

The first four minutes in a business encounter—the way the client is greeted, the way the waiting room looks, even the colors, light level, and odors of the room—contribute significantly to how much customers will like the service they get. The best product is unlikely to survive a negative first impression. My father once said we should ask ourselves, "Would I want to do business with somebody who looks, acts, and talks like me?"

Every Employee Is a P.R. Specialist

Every member of a group represents that group. *Everyone* connected with a business, even the floor sweeper and the receptionist's boyfriend who hangs around the front desk waiting to take her to lunch, is an active member of that firm's Public Relations Department.

As both a hairstylist and, now, a professional speaker, I am constantly trying to make my clients' experience with me pleasant. I learned the value of this at age fifteen from my first boss, Mr. Paul. He treated every woman, while she was in our shop, as though she were the only person in the world. And he saw to it that everyone in his organization treated his customers with the same respect.

Later in San Francisco, I heard a story with a similar moral from one of my customers, Al Stanton. He had worked in the traffic department of the Zellerbach Paper Company early in his career. Isadore Zellerbach, the founder of the company, was a very personable man who believed in making all of his employees feel important. Zellerbach frequently asked Al's advice on different matters. Al was puzzled that such an important man would be concerned with the opinions of even the lowest employees, but Zellerbach explained why all his employees needed to feel they were part of the company.

Early in the history of the company, a Zellerbach truck was following a rather fancy car on a narrow road. The truck driver was impatient to pass and kept honking. After about fifteen minutes, when he finally did pass, he put his head out the window and said, "You @%&!* You want to take up the whole road?" Then he roared off, the Zellerbach name all over the truck.

The gentleman driving the car was the owner of the company that was Zellerbach's best customer in the area. When he returned to his office, furious, he ordered the purchasing department to cancel all orders with Zellerbach and never to buy anything from the company again.

It was several months before this lost account came to the attention of Mr. Zellerbach. Trying to get the former client on the phone proved fruitless, so Zellerbach went to the company to talk to this man in person. When he heard about the Zellerbach truck incident, he was shocked—shocked that he had overlooked one of the most important factors in his business, that absolutely every employee represents the company. From that time on, Zellerbach's truck drivers received lessons in politeness and human relations.

Often the people we deal with are not the company executives but the average worker. He or she is still a powerful salesperson for the company. For example, I have absolutely nothing but wonderful things to say about the former Jack Tar Hotel (now the Cathedral Hill Hotel) in San Francisco, not because of the management, not because of the banquet facilities, but because of a bellman named Norman, who made presenting a seminar in that hotel so much fun. Norman was truly a wonderful person—a great salesman!

Similarly, I used to eat breakfast at the Pepper Mill Restaurant in Serramonte, near San Francisco. My friends and I would regularly race in at seven in the morning to have breakfast. There was a waitress there named Judy, and what a pleasure she was to see bright and early in the morning. One Christmas, I was pleasantly surprised to see that she had brought little Christmas presents for her regular customers.

Our experience with that waitress affected our impression of that entire chain of restaurants. The experience with the bellman reflected on that particular hotel. The experience of one man with a truck driver influenced his relationship to an entire company. That's why there is nothing more important to an organization than hiring the best people to represent the company and then helping all of them to recognize their role as a public relations specialist.

The Most Expensive Worker

One worker's poor performance can cost a company incalculable losses in both dollars and goodwill. I found that out when I went to buy my first car at the age of twenty- nine. Knowing absolutely nothing about cars, I spoke to a few clients and friends, who convinced me that I should get one of three makes. One Wednesday afternoon, determined to buy a car, I walked into the first dealership, met a friendly young salesman, and announced, "I wish to buy a car. I want a hatchback, and I want to pay cash. How much is this one?" He told me and took me out for a drive. We laughed, joked, and had a good time. He said, "I understand you're shopping around. This is how much it will be. If you're interested, come back and see me."

Strolling down the street, I came to the second dealer. I said, "Good afternoon. I would like to buy a car. I want to pay cash and I want a hatchback. How much?" They informed me that they did not have a hatchback. I thanked them, and continued on to the third dealership.

I should have guessed what was about to happen as the salesman walked toward me. His hair was totally disheveled and a cigar butt was hanging out of his mouth. In the friendliest possible way, I said, "Good afternoon. I would like to buy a car. I want to pay cash and I want a hatchback. How much is this one?" I turned to a glistening model on my left. His reply was gruff: "Look at the sticker price, lady."

No sticker was in sight. Here I was prepared to write a check for whatever the car cost (if it had been the one I wanted), and the salesman couldn't even be polite. I enjoy spending money. I enjoy listening to a good sales presentation. And I like people to appreciate my business. But I will not pay money to someone who is not civil and does not make the transaction enjoyable. Turning on my heels, without looking at the sticker price, I walked out of the showroom and bought a car from the helpful salesperson back at dealership number one. Certainly, the car offered by that third dealer is an excellent car. The company probably spends many millions of dollars each year on advertising. But I will never buy one.

My friend Chris Hegarty also had a bad experience with car salesmen. He stopped early one morning at a car dealer on "automobile row" in San Francisco, sincerely interested in buying. All the salesmen were huddled in a corner. One came over to Chris and said, "I'm sorry. I can't help you. We're having a sales meeting."

Companies both large and small spend a fortune promoting their image to the public. Yet it takes only one person to ruin that image. Management's biggest concern today is to make all employees, including the filing clerk, the janitor, and the stockclerk, realize the important part they play in the company's plans. A manager's biggest problem is to help the lesser-paid employees understand their roles in the bigger picture, and to boost their self-image by demonstrating how much they contribute to the company's success.

"Little" People, Big Jobs

What about the so-called little people? The ones who answer the phones and type the letters? The people who greet guests at hotels and make the beds? They are probably the biggest public relations department in any company, yet some managers think, "Well, we don't pay them much. They're not going to be around long enough to worry about their contribution to our image."

A major chain of jewelers that I worked with wanted to monitor customer service. They sent shoppers into their stores to report on their experiences. Without exception, the problems were always with the part-time employee or the new person. And what did the managers say? "Well, you can't expect the part-time person to be as good as the full-time person."

"Why not?" I asked. "If they're not, they're going to lose customers for you!"

As my friend and fellow speaker Jim Cathcart puts it, "Sales is an attitude, not a department." A furniture representative told me of a friend of his who owned a furniture store. A nice young salesman used to call on him regularly once a month. Because the store was in a hard-to-reach, outlying area of Oklahoma, and because the salesman was always cheerful and always took time to call on him, the owner felt bad that he couldn't give the salesman any business.

One day the owner decided that the next time the young man came in, he would place an order. The salesman arrived. The owner said, "I want to talk to you. Can you wait? A customer has just come in?" He dealt with the customer for half an hour, and then returned to the young salesman.

By this time the owner had decided *not* to buy anything from the salesman. Why? Because during that fateful half hour, the young man had sat reading a newspaper. He hadn't bothered to walk around the store to find out what it had in stock. His lack of initiative and real interest cost him the sale.

Your Worst Employee

"Your business is only as good as your worst employee." When I first heard that, my whole philosophy of business changed. Think about it. In a small business, everybody counts. Perhaps in a big company, you can hide people or ship them off to Podunk. But even then, they can still have a negative effect.

My brother has founded and managed several rock groups, in addition to playing in top rock bands. He insists you can ensure being able to handle problems when they arise "if your staff are fairly paid and well-treated," because "they will react positively when a problem comes up. But if you shout at your staff, if you underpay them, if you let them know that they'll be sacked if they make a mistake, they'll leave as soon as trouble starts . . . if not sooner."

Hiring the Right People

Good employees rarely appear by magic. They are usually the product of good hiring practices. I started hiring better people when I figured out what I was *actually looking for*. To do this, I began by making two lists. The first was a list of what I *had* to have from the people I hired. The second list covered what it would be nice to have.

Once I hired a woman only because she had been recommended to me by someone who had supervised her as a waitress. My new employee had been to beauty school. I assumed that if she were a good cocktail waitress, she would be a good hairstylist, since both must know how to deal properly with the public. I didn't ask her some of the questions that I now know to ask. Later I found out that, as a student, she had asked other people to clock her in and out of beauty school so she could accumulate enough hours for certification. Her attitude was, "What can they teach me?" This attitude didn't change when she came to work for me. I still had a lot to learn about hiring. No employee will ever be perfect, but there are faults you can work with and faults you can't.

Questions for Prospective Employees

1. *Tell me about yourself. All the exciting and interesting things.*

People offer revealing replies to that question. So many people, even top executives, say, "Oh, there's nothing exciting about me." You find out about people's self-esteem when they answer that question.

2. *If you could wave a magic wand and create a perfect environment to work in, what would it be like?*

Suppose the potential employee answers, "I don't like to have someone breathing down my neck. I like to be left on my own, to make up my mind how to do things." You know immediately that this is the wrong person for a job that's heavily supervised.

If the person says, "Well, I like to work by myself in my own space," and the employee must share a crowded workspace with others whose personalities may conflict, you know you are likely to have an unhappy employee.

Even when a quiet, personable individual replies, "I like to work with people but I would rather have my own space," my experience shows that the work area quickly becomes a private domain. Would you put someone like that to work in a small space where people have to walk by to get to the coffee machine? If you do, the employee probably won't last in the job — or won't do the job well.

3. *Describe the best boss you ever had. What made him or her so special? Describe the worst boss.*

If the description of the worst boss sounds anything like me, I know that person won't be happy working with me.

4. *What's your hobby?*

There are also questions the law does not allow an employer to ask, whether a person is married, for instance. But I needed to know something about a person's private life because I had to know if he or she could be at work by eight o'clock sharp. I asked people what they do when they are not working. I asked about their hobbies. I knew that if someone liked disco dancing five nights a week, he or she might not show up bright and early.

Firing Your Mistakes

Someone in one of my workshops said, "It isn't a mistake until it gets out of the shop." Within every company there's a lot of room for legitimate experimentation. But there's a big difference between constructive risk taking and outright incompetence.

When the former cocktail waitress had worked for me for several weeks, I realized I had made a mistake. I hadn't interviewed her properly. She wasn't what I expected. One day I said to her, "I made a mistake. I'm very sorry. I apologize to you. I shouldn't have hired you, but I'm not prepared to live with my mistake any longer. You're fired." She cried and said, "No one has ever fired me." I said, "It is my responsibility. I'm really sorry. I shouldn't have hired you." This experience taught me something important: I don't have to live with my mistakes.

Whether hiring or being hired, we need to realize how we — or the potential employee — fit the organization and how well the organization fits us. When I was in Norfolk, Virginia, speaking to the Sales and Marketing Executives Club there, a gentleman came up to me afterward and said, "I lost a $10,000 order because a client came into our facility and spoke to the shipping clerk while I was down the street. The shipping clerk accused the client of stealing his pen!" (Now, no employer should allow his employees to be harassed or intimidated in the name of good customer relations, but this was a faulty value call on the part of the clerk. Everyone has walked off with someone else's pen occasionally — all you have to do is politely ask for it back or chalk the thirty-nine cents up to public relations costs.)

Good managers understand how important the people under them are. In Joe Heitz's philosophy (which extends well beyond the working world), "Be a part of the whole rather than the whole yourself." He means that Heitz Cellars winery is *all* the employees, not just him.

The Waitress Who Should Have Been a Manager

The quality of work in every company would improve if all employees realized their own importance to the overall public relations picture. Once, in Nashville, I was part of a group that represented a waitress's nightmare. Six of us descended on a hotel coffee shop, deep in conversation. No one wanted anything exactly as it was presented on the menu. Without meaning to be rude or difficult, we kept asking the waitress to change this or that, all the time continuing our animated conversation.

As she took our orders the waitress was very friendly and patient. At the end of our meal I said, "My dear, this is going to be worth your while. We're all big tippers." The waitress said something I've never forgotten: "I'm not being nice to you for a tip. I don't care if you don't give me a tip. I just feel that if we give you good service, your group will bring your business back to our hotel next year and not to the competition."

That impressed me. I came back to San Francisco and wrote a letter to the hotel manager:

Dear Sir:

I am a motivational speaker and I travel nationwide talking about good and bad service. I would like to congratulate you on all your staff. They were superb, but especially our waitress.

I related the tale, and finished:

Sir, I do not know what you did to motivate your people, but keep doing it. It works.

During the next eighteen months I received no reply from the management of the Hyatt Regency. In telling this story, as I often did, I hinted that perhaps the waitress should have been a manager — she, I figured, would have the sense to acknowledge a compliment.

Then, in May of 1981, at the Sales and Marketing Executives International Convention at the Fairmont Hotel in San Francisco, a woman approached me after my speech. "I am friendly with the management of the Hyatt Regency in Nashville," she said. "There is a new manager and that wouldn't happen now."

The next day, when I arrived at my office, there was a message from a man in Nashville about the letter I had written eighteen months before. I asked my assistant to call him and acknowledge his call, but before she could do that, the phone rang. He was calling to say, "I just wanted you to know that we have new management and I assure you that if you were to write a nice letter now, I would reply to it. Please stop telling the story."

I told him I couldn't possibly stop because it was too good a story. However, I promised to add a footnote — that the new management phoned immediately when they heard the story. We laughed together.

Pretend You're the Customer

People who concentrate on giving good service always get more personal satisfaction as well as better business. How can we get better service? One way is by trying to see ourselves as others do.

Dr. Dru Scott, in her seminar "Winning With Customers," tells about how a group of public utility employees found out why their customers so often seemed confused and irritated. They went outside the building, then walked in, pretending they were customers.

"We really got into it," one employee reported later. "First, we noticed there were no clear signs in the parking area telling people where to go. A tree had grown in front of our one sign. We stood in line and timed how long that took, and then guessed how it would feel to be sent to another window after waiting in the wrong line. We immediately saw how we could take steps to make our customers feel better about being there. We talked about making a 'customer walk' part of the job of our bosses every month."

Mike Vance, in his lecture "Adventures in Creative Thinking," talks about going over your business environment with your five senses — the feel, sights, sounds, smells, and tastes of what the customer encounters. After hearing Mike describe "five-sensing," I discussed it with my employees. Then we walked through every area of our salon, observing everything the clients saw, heard, felt, smelled, and tasted. We asked questions like: Does the coffee always taste fresh? — How can we get rid of the smell of the chemicals we occasionally use? — Is this chair comfortable to sit in?

A dentist who specialized in children's care also heard Mike Vance's lecture. He went back to his office and walked around on his hands and knees, seeing what the experience of his office would be for a person the height of a child. Afterward he lowered the counter so that even a very small person could see over it. He started asking children what they liked and disliked, and he worked with their ideas. He put photos of the dental hygienists on a board with a list of their interests, such as kite flying and skiing, so the child could choose the hygienist with whom he had the most in common. After giving his patients a questionnaire, this dentist found that many were afraid of the instruments, so he explained exactly what he was going to do with each one. He also gave each young patient a photo of himself. He made going to the dentist a different experience and so much fun that all the children told their friends about him. In one year his practice grew so much that he needed several partners just to handle it all — a perfect example of how creative thinking and concentrating on serving clients can result in a better business and a substantial increase in income.

Five-sense your own environment. See what others see. Hear what others hear, taste what they taste, smell what they smell, as a stranger would. After people work in an organization for a couple of months, they no longer see their environment. I have walked into executives' offices with thick carpets and a big expensive desk covered with stale cigarette butts. I don't think people should smoke, but the point is that in this day and age nonsmokers are not unusual. It's just common sense to empty the ashtrays once in a while. If these executives ever sat in their own reception rooms, they would understand why people are impatient after five minutes.

To learn these things about our businesses, we need feedback from our clients, customers, and employees. And occasionally we need to take a "customer walk," five-sensing our environment.

Handling Goof-ups

Even in the best-run business there will be mistakes and complaints. The secret is to learn from them and get on with business, rather than stopping to assign blame and punish the culprit. Making a customer feel bad, even when the error is probably his, doesn't make for good business.

Once I went to lunch with twenty-nine other people during a seminar in Southern California. We walked into the large, half-empty, Mexican restaurant at 12:15 and told the woman at the reservation desk that we had a luncheon reservation for 12:30. She shouted angrily at us that our reservation had been for 12:00!

Now, we were giving that restaurant thirty customers. Even if she genuinely believed we were fifteen minutes late, we were still buying thirty lunches. Yet she insisted on chastising us loudly to "prove" the error had not been hers. We could have turned around and walked out, but that would have made us late for the afternoon session. After such an introduction, the best food in the world would probably be indigestible.

Still irritated, I went back to my hairstyling shop and told my staff, "I don't ever want to hear you tell a customer, 'You're late'—even though they sometimes are. It's better to say, 'We are a little behind schedule. Let's get moving.'" That shares the responsibility rather than making anyone feel bad. The customer may have been stuck in rush-hour traffic. More likely than not, he is frazzled already, and to come in and be shouted at isn't going to help.

Troubleshooting at Home

Mornings are absolutely not the time for reality. They need to be positive, an affirmation of love and support, not "Oh, my God, it's raining" or "It smells like the kids burnt down the garage."

When we come home in the evening, we have to create the right environment before we can talk about the problems of the day. When I was working with AT&T in Morristown, New Jersey, I had dinner with the gentleman who had hired me and and his wife. She had an hour-and-a-half commute each way on her job. We were talking about setting the tone in the evening, and she suddenly said to Robert, "You know, when I walk in in the evening, the first thing you say is, 'How was your day?'"

He said, "I'm really interested."

She said, "Yes, but after an hour and a half on the train I don't feel like telling you."

Couples need to negotiate the best way to start the evening positively. Perhaps it's to say no more than "hello" when you walk in, then going to unwind by soaking in a bubble bath, changing clothes, or puttering in the garden before beginning meaningful conversation. So often we get involved in arguments that are just kick-the-dog syndrome. They are caused by frustrations with the events of the day, not by any problem at home.

Remember what a home is supposed to be: a haven from the outside world. "In the evening," says psychologist Luann Lindquist, "we have to consider sympathy or solution." Go for the sympathy first. So often a supportive mate tries to solve the problems of the day and starts a row instead because what the other person really needs is sympathy. Listen first. Then, when calm is restored, offer solutions.

YOUR ASSIGNMENT:
The Impression Your Working Environment Makes

1. Do I understand the philosophy behind my company?

2. Do I realize what statement we want to make in the business community?

3. What do I see when I walk into my working environment?

4. What do I hear?

5. What do I smell?

6. What do I touch?

7. What do I taste?

8. How do the personnel relate to one another and to clients?

9. What things should be changed?

10. Whose help do I need to make these changes?

11. When will I start?

CHAPTER 12

Working Smarter

A gifted concert violinist was complimented after the conclusion of a particularly moving performance. "That was absolutely wonderful," said the admirer. "I'd give my life to be able to play like that." "I did," replied the artist.

In a little town in New Jersey, a priest looked out his window one morning and saw a great crowd coming down the street. In their midst was a beautiful, bearded man with flowing white robes and a shepherd's staff. People were bringing him glasses of water, and when he waved his hand over them, the water turned to wine.

The priest raced to the phone and called the Pope. (You didn't know he had an 800 number?) Breathlessly, he described the scene. "Your Holiness, what should I do?"

The Pope thought for a moment. "Look busy," he replied. "It could be the Boss."

How many people go to work and look busy? We all know such people—and know as well that there is no substitute for actually doing the job. No matter what our situation in life, all of us have to do *something*. *What* we choose to do labels us. *How* we choose to do it defines us.

How the Smart Guys Do It

Smart workers come in all colors, shapes, and sizes, but they have certain characteristics in common:

They share.

They make an effort.

They are persistent.

They are "lucky."

They share.

At a seminar I attended, Jim Rohn suggested that poor people should take rich people to dinner. The idea is that if you can get successful people to sit down and talk for a couple of hours, they may just let slip some of the reasons and ideas that made them successful.

Sharing ideas usually results in mutual goodwill and effective networking. I encourage salespeople, entrepreneurs — anybody with common interests — to set up their own *mastermind alliances* to brainstorm ideas or trade leads. I belong to the Continental Breakfast Club, a group of dynamic businesswomen who meet every two weeks to hear a speaker. It's a fabulous way to start the day. (Breakfast meetings cost less money than lunch or dinner, have a built-in time limit, and send everyone off to work energized.)

"Not for Twice the Money"

Helping others to develop doesn't detract from you — it helps you grow. For example, Evie Talmus worked for me when I first opened my salon in San Francisco. She worked hard, and on weekends started a little breakfast-in-bed delivery service. Bagels were her specialty. The business quickly grew. Eventually she opened a take-out food store, then a New York-style deli in San Francisco, and is currently in charge of the restaurants for Western Athletic Clubs. When I went to her opening party, she said, "Patricia, I could not have done this if I hadn't worked for you and learned things from you that I use every day." In this same way, I feel I use ideas every day in business that I learned from celebrity hairstylist Jay Sebring in 1969 — even though I am now in an entirely different business.

When Evie had worked in my salon, she brought in a lot of customers for us by hitchhiking to work. One day she got a ride and gave her sales presentation to a man who managed a beauty supply company. He offered her a job as a salesperson at double the salary I was paying her. She said, "You're going to think I'm crazy, but I love my job and haven't learned all I can yet. I'm not ready to leave, even for twice the money. I would be embarrassed to tell you what I earn because I'm turning you down."

Evie's refusal was not only loyalty to me, but an investment in her future because she was learning how to run a small business. She left my shop with my encouragement and support, then applied what she had learned to her own business. When you help people grow, they help you grow. Now Evie is doing well, I'm in a new business, and we support each other.

Doing What Spiders Do

Many of my friends ask me how I manage to get so much media and press attention. I always reply that for fifteen years I've been actively promoting myself. And sure enough, I have received many requests for speaking engagements from people who have read one of the articles — a perfect example of how the "spider web" works.

The spider-web concept involves doing things, being active, getting out there and being visible in your community — *not for a payoff but as a way of life*. With the spider-web concept, you keep promoting and you keep doing, and you believe in the "law of sow and reap." What you sow will come back to you. For example, I refer business to many of my friends, who then wonder what they can do for me. I also recommend others to handle my overflow speaking engagements. I'm not doing it for any particular payoff. I'm doing it because that's what you do. You must take an unselfish approach to promoting. You must share the wealth.

Making Bigger Pies

The reason the National Speakers Association is so successful is because Cavett Robert and Merlin Cundiff had the idea of a "bigger pie." The bigger-pie idea doesn't mean that everyone should have smaller pieces of the same pie, but that the pie becomes larger because it is shared. When we work together, we increase the size of what we share.

A lot of critics in America will claim that today's economic climate is too dangerous for the small-business person. As Adam Smith states in *Paper Money*, "Once again the problems seem bigger than men's abilities to solve them. The optimistic credo, the vision of men as responsible and capable, acting in benign self-interest, has faded, to be replaced by a smaller, less confident, more flinty-eyed world view." Sharing is the first step to reversing this limited, limiting view.

They make an effort.

It is true that things aren't exactly easy. There are many risks inherent in starting your own venture. But, coming from England as I have, I can honestly say that America's business opportunities tower over those in other countries of the world. With energy, drive, and enthusiasm, you can accomplish wonders.

When I first came to America from England, I could bring only $500 with me. (I thought it was a fortune at the time, just as I thought everybody in America was rich.) I expected everyone here to be working exceptionally hard to attain the luxurious lifestyles my friends in England did not enjoy. But many people in America don't exert this above-average effort. I did, and although I would not say it's easy to be successful here, it is easier than it is in England.

One hairstylist friend of mine who has taken advantage of opportunities and put out above-average effort is Daniel Gianfrancesco, who has represented the United States in world hairstyling championships in about two hundred contests. At the beginning he placed second a few times, but since then he has placed first for years. Acclaimed as one of the best hairstylists in the world, Daniel practices sixty hours a week in preparation for a national competition. Why this total dedication? He says, "At thirteen I wanted to be not just a hairstylist, but I wanted to be the very best." He has worked overtime for his success in a world where few are committed to excellence.

When you have the urge to excel, you soon notice how few others dedicate themselves to the necessary level of commitment. What constantly dismays me even now, however, is that so many people fail to take advantage of this country's opportunities. I'm certainly neither the smartest nor the best-educated person in the world. Yet, with my determined attitude and drive, I transformed my $500 into a successful hairstyling establishment and then an ever-growing career in public speaking.

Activity or Accomplishment?

Top motivational speaker Zig Ziglar from Dallas tells of a scientist who experimented with a group of "processionary" caterpillars (so-called because they follow each other head-to-tail almost indefinitely). Inside a flowerpot the scientist placed the caterpillars' favorite food, pine needles. Then he set them down in a circle around the flowerpot. Do you know, those caterpillars went round and round the pot, following each other's tails, until they literally dropped dead from exhaustion and hunger? Yet they were only inches from food that would have saved them.

The same can be true of us when we confuse activity with accomplishment. That's where "working smarter" comes in. Ask yourself daily, "Is this the best possible way I can do this task? Will doing this get me nearer to my final goal?"

The Way to Carnegie Hall

What we need to be successful in our lives and our businesses is total commitment — commitment to each other, commitment to our companies and our organizations, and commitment to ourselves to become the person we are capable of becoming. Realtor Bob Jansen, violinist of the Milwaukee Symphony, has been playing for over twenty-five years and still practices in his spare time. "Not to get better," he says, "but to keep from getting worse."

And I remember when my brother was first accumulating gold albums with his group, King Crimson. Popular as they were, he practiced eight hours a week whenever he wasn't playing on the road. He explained to me, "Well, it's one thing to get a great reputation. It's a whole different thing to keep it."

"You're Crazy"

It takes hard work and concentration to keep a good reputation. And there are lots of people who think that anyone who works that hard must be crazy.

When I used to lecture at barber schools, I said, "You have to be above average. That doesn't necessarily mean you have to be that much better, although it helps. It just means being a little nicer to your customers, being business-minded as well as promotion-minded." I have seen great hairstylists who didn't care about the people the hair was attached to. More important, I have seen good hairstylists with great personalities who succeeded where others who were better technicians didn't.

When hiring anyone — a speaker, doctor, dentist, or hairstylist — if you find two people of similar ability, you're going to return to the person you like. If you can make the things you have to do (like having your hair cut or going to a dentist) as pleasant as possible, life is going to be better. Anyone providing a service to people needs to do more than the next person.

As Charles Darwin once said, "I have always maintained that, excepting fools, men did not differ much in intellect, only in zeal and hard work." I certainly agree and will take Mr. Darwin a step further. Our effort alone can generate confidence — in ourselves as well as in others. Our effort, in fact, becomes a positive way of communicating with those around us.

They are persistent.

Two men were sitting on their respective roofs during a flood. One noticed a straw hat floating by. A couple of minutes later it floated by in the other direction. Then it switched directions again. "Hey, Charlie," said the man, "are my eyes playing tricks on me, or is that straw hat floating back and forth?" Charlie replied, "Don't worry. That's Uncle Henry. He said that come hell or high water, he was going to mow the lawn this afternoon." That is the sort of persistence and determination I have tried to maintain.

Two Brothers Who Didn't Give Up

The father of Al and Herb Hops came to the United States from Poland, where he had been a tailor. As soon as he could, Papa Hops opened his own shop in Oakland. He told his sons, "Whatever you do, go into business for yourself. If it ever comes to a crunch in a company, and it's the owners or you, they have to look after themselves first."

His son Al was a top salesperson with 3M and a manager at the Savin Company. He was comfortable, successful, and had plenty of time for recreation. Then he gave it all up to go into business for himself.

Al says, "Although I was successful, there was always something missing. I had more ideas than I could possibly implement in the structure of these companies." He saw what was revolutionizing the country — the computer microchip — and decided, "I've got to get involved with this."

Now Al's company, Future Living Systems, is a leader in the building of "intelligent homes," a revolution that will affect people's lives at home as much as the telephone or electricity did when they were first introduced. Al and his brother, Herb, are building the first "intelligent" condominiums in the United States, condos whose computer systems control not only utilities and security, but offer banking, shopping, stock trading, and even university degrees.

Herb Hops, a millionaire Southern California builder, believes that "there are many people who have talent and yet are never successful," basically because they lack confidence and perseverance.

"Confidence," says Herb, "means knowing you will succeed no matter what the obstacles. I have been asked many times why I seem so confident about all the things I do and how others can develop the same type of confidence. I always tell them the same thing: Confidence is developed by hard work and dedication."

Herb says perseverance means believing in yourself and refusing to give up. "After working for a large company for twelve years, I moved my family and myself in 1969 to Southern California near the world-famous LaCosta Health Spa to sell real estate and build houses full time. Unfortunately, I got involved with a man who was unreliable. I presold the houses and even got loans for people, but then the deals would fail to close because my partner did not pay the subcontractors. I wound up having to pay them out of my own pocket. However, I knew that if I held out, things would turn around. In 1973, things did turn and I was on my way.

"But in 1974, the recession hit and again I was close to going broke. But once more, I drew upon my faith and persevered. By 1976, things had turned around again. Then, believe it or not, we were hit with both another housing recession and a sewer moratorium which limited new building. By this time, I had overcome adversity so many times, I knew I would once more survive." And once again, Herb Hops did survive.

The Way to the Boss's Office

In my own case, I developed an attitude that "persistence pays" because of my father's business career in England. In the 1920s my father supported himself as a farmer's hired hand. He worked seven days a week and received six shillings a week (well under a dollar), with an extra shilling on Sundays. He worked hard for several farmers at this wage, living with the hired hands in barn attics and similarly close quarters.

One day my father spoke to a local businessman and told him he wanted desperately to work in an office. The man told my father to learn shorthand and typing. My father wanted to know how that would help him. The man replied, "It isn't the skills themselves. It's the fact that they will take you into the boss's office."

Determined, my father went to night school for two years to learn these office skills. He pumped gas in the daytime to pay for his education. Finally, he got a position in a real estate office for twenty-five shillings a week (just over two dollars). He was an eager man and a fast learner. The two partners were glad to have him aboard.

However, the partnership soon began to dissolve. The owners did not know how to repay the three or four hundred pounds that they owed to various creditors. Although my father had only five pounds in the bank, he offered to assume responsibility for the debts if the partners gave him the business.

The feuding duo liked this idea, so off they went, leaving my inexperienced father to deal with the mass of creditors and bills. Being an honest, hard-working man, my father went to each creditor and said, "I've taken over this business and I certainly owe you money. I haven't a lot of experience. If you sue the old owners for the money, you won't get it because they haven't got it. Take a chance with me and I'll repay you as soon as I can."

The creditors all agreed. That was my father's beginning. Within a few years, he had not only repaid the debt, but he had made one of the biggest land deals in the county. With luck — which comes mostly from taking advantage of the opportunities your problems present — and hard work, he made it past many tribulations, including a war-torn English economy, to become a very successful businessman.

With my father as an example, my success was just a matter of time and effort. I have learned that if you stick to a good plan of action, you largely account for your own success, you make your own luck.

They are "lucky."

In the seventeenth century, a French merchant was accused of witchcraft by his neighbors. His business prospered and he grew steadily richer while they struggled to get along. "This man has made a pact with the devil to have such good luck when we have none," they cried. "He should be burned at the stake and his property forfeited to us."

The king, Louis XIV, sent one of his ministers to discover the truth of the charge. The minister knocked on the man's door in the middle of the night — the merchant lived over his shop — and asked to make a small purchase. The merchant immediately got out of bed, rushed downstairs, and cheerfully opened his shop. The sale completed, the merchant thanked the customer and returned to bed.

The minister reported all this to the king who laughed. "This is no witchcraft! This man makes his own good luck!" The charges were dismissed.

For many years Max Gunther, author of *The Luck Factor*, has studied people who are "lucky." He has found specific traits that constitute the "luck factor."

Gunther compares lucky people to a spider: "A spider strings many lines to catch passing flies and the bigger her web, the better she eats. So it is with those who would catch good luck. In general . . . the luckiest men and women are those who have taken the trouble to form a great many friendly contacts with other people."

This helps in business. Joseph Baim, president of Markham Products, Inc., the company I demonstrated for when I owned my salon, was attending a packaging convention at a seaside resort. At the time there was a very popular product called PPT that had been designed for the Redken Company. It was a marvelous hair reconstructer, and no matter what product line people carried in their barbershops or beauty shops, they always had some PPT because it worked magic. For years, Mr. Baim had wanted to find someone who could make a product as good as PPT.

During the convention, the friendly Mrs. Baim struck up a conversation with a woman on the beach and the two decided to go out to dinner that night with their husbands. It turned out that the woman's husband was the man who invented PPT for Redken. He now had his own manufacturing company and was free to make a product for Baim that rivaled PPT. This may seem like pure luck, but, given Mrs. Baim's characteristically outgoing personality, the resulting success she helped bring to her husband became possible if not inevitable.

In Gunther's words, "These people make themselves known to many other people, usually without thinking about it. They're gregarious. They go out of their way to be friendly. They talk to strangers, they're joyous meeters and greeters. If they sit next to someone on an airplane, they start a conversation. The guy who sells them their morning newspaper is more than just a face." People of this type put the odds in their favor. They lay the groundwork to have luck come their way.

And luck, as you can see, is a combination of the other three characteristics of smart workers: sharing, effort, and persistence.

YOUR ASSIGNMENT:
Working Smarter

"There is only one thing more painful than learning by experience: that is not learning from experience."

Archibald MacLeish

1. What is the most important lesson I have learned?

2. What is the most recent lesson?

3. Am I in the habit of learning from others?

4. When I walk into other people's businesses, am I open to learning from them?

5. Do I consider myself a business consultant for my own business?

6. Do I ask my manager what he/she thinks?

7. Do I ask the people around me what they think and know?

8. How many books have I read in the past year?

9. In the last year how many cassettes have I listened to and how many seminars have I attended?

10. Am I committed to growth on a daily basis?

11. What have I learned from hard times?

12. Who is the most surprising successful person I know? Why?

13. What can I learn from this person?

14. What is the best decision I have made about my career?

15. What was the process I went through to make that decision?

Can I Succeed?

People in positions of authority need to be self-critical without being self-deprecating. Judging oneself realistically and being open to feedback are essential to any leader.

	Yes	No
1. Do I have plenty of drive?	[ ]	[ ]
2. Do I accept responsibility cheerfully?	[ ]	[ ]
3. Do I believe that success is not an accident?	[ ]	[ ]
4. Do I know that the customer is my real boss?	[ ]	[ ]
5. Do I look, listen, and learn daily?	[ ]	[ ]
6. Do I find out the answer when I am not sure?	[ ]	[ ]
7. Do I set an example for others?	[ ]	[ ]

	Yes	No
8. Do I realize that my neighbor's lawn only *seems* greener?	[ ]	[ ]
9. Do I welcome new ideas?	[ ]	[ ]
10. Do I profit by my mistakes?	[ ]	[ ]
11. Do I speak clearly and convincingly?	[ ]	[ ]
12. Am I careful to share the credit?	[ ]	[ ]
13. Do I cooperate with the people I work with?	[ ]	[ ]
14. Do I realize that my future is my own responsibility?	[ ]	[ ]
15. Do I think things through thoroughly before acting?	[ ]	[ ]
16. Do I believe good manners are good business?	[ ]	[ ]
17. Do I realize the world does not owe me a living?	[ ]	[ ]
18. Am I willing to go the "extra mile"?	[ ]	[ ]
19. Am I careful with my finances?	[ ]	[ ]
20. Do I revise my goals frequently?	[ ]	[ ]

	Yes	No
21. Do I realize that everything worth having has a price tag of some sort?	[ ]	[ ]
22. Do I have a lifestyle that keeps me physically and mentally fit?	[ ]	[ ]
23. Do I always appear enthusiastic even when I don't feel like it?	[ ]	[ ]
24. Do I make others feel important?	[ ]	[ ]
25. Do I always try to help my superiors?	[ ]	[ ]
26. Do I always try to help those I supervise?	[ ]	[ ]
27. Do I control my temper?	[ ]	[ ]
28. Do I consider work a privilege and not a chore?	[ ]	[ ]
29. Am I my own honest critic?	[ ]	[ ]
30. Do I remember the good things other people have done for me?	[ ]	[ ]

Getting the Most Out of My Job

"Most people would probably be successful if they carried to their jobs the same enthusiasm they have for getting ahead in traffic."

Earl Nightingale

	Yes	No
1. Do I take time to think?	[ ]	[ ]
2. Am I always thorough?	[ ]	[ ]
3. Do I cooperate as well as I should?	[ ]	[ ]
4. Do I give and take orders cheerfully?	[ ]	[ ]
5. Do I always finish what I start?	[ ]	[ ]
6. Do I take the time to get the necessary facts?	[ ]	[ ]
7. Do I take time to plan?	[ ]	[ ]
8. Do I know about my company philosophy?	[ ]	[ ]
9. Am I good at explanations?	[ ]	[ ]
10. Am I usually concise?	[ ]	[ ]
11. Do I take the time to listen?	[ ]	[ ]
12. Do I answer questions thoroughly?	[ ]	[ ]

	Yes	No
13. Do I always put first things first?	[ ]	[ ]
14. Do I admit my mistakes and correct them?	[ ]	[ ]
15. Am I usually on time?	[ ]	[ ]
16. Am I neat?	[ ]	[ ]
17. Am I courteous?	[ ]	[ ]
18. Do I take the time to understand and make friends of people I work with?	[ ]	[ ]
19. Am I tolerant?	[ ]	[ ]
20. Do I always *try* to do my best?	[ ]	[ ]
21. Am I patient?	[ ]	[ ]
22. Am I efficient?	[ ]	[ ]
23. Do I write things down so I don't forget them?	[ ]	[ ]
24. Do I usually look for the best in people and avoid gossip?	[ ]	[ ]
25. Do I live up to my promises?	[ ]	[ ]

	Yes	No
26. Do I always say "thank you" when appropriate?	[ ]	[ ]
27. Am I enthusiastic?	[ ]	[ ]
28. Do I always smile?	[ ]	[ ]
29. Do I consider self-improvement necessary?	[ ]	[ ]
30. Am I sensible about my health?	[ ]	[ ]
31. Do I take time to relax?	[ ]	[ ]
32. Do I take time to understand the functions of my job?	[ ]	[ ]

CHAPTER 13

Make Success a Habit

> *Pale soul, consumed by fear*
> *Of the living world you haunt,*
> *Have you learned what habits lead you*
> *To hunt what you do not want?*
>
> William D. Snodgrass

> *"I can resist everything except temptation."*
>
> Oscar Levant

Our habits are part of us, built up like the layers of a pearl from our own juices. They can either provide a lustrous shield against adversity — or a prison of our own making. Just a few habits can make a big difference in both how we handle and how we project ourselves. What new habits do you want to acquire? What old habits do you want to change?

Habit or Commitment?

A pig and a chicken were watching people enter the unemployment office. "You know, we should do something nice for those people," said the pig. The chicken replied, "Yeah, let's give them some breakfast, some ham and eggs." The pig said, "That's all right for you to say. For you it's a contribution. For me it's a total commitment." If you want to develop new habits, you're going to have to do more than contribute some eggs.

Ken Blanchard, who wrote *The One Minute Manager*, says, "People who want to develop new habits should notice how they describe their goal. Do they say they are interested in it? Or do they have a commitment? If you are *interested* in your health, then you go to the gym when the weather's nice and your friends are willing to go. But if you *have a commitment*, you go whether you feel like it or not, no matter how late you got in the night before, and whether your pals are going with you or not."

Do you have an "interest in" or a "commitment to" achieving your goals and developing good work habits?

Five Steps to New Habits

You have a choice: to improve by experimenting with new ideas, or to continue doing comfortable things that don't work. If you choose the former, here is what it requires.

1. *Make up your mind*. Be committed to making the change. For instance, you decide you're going to plan the following day before you go to bed, or you will only complain to people who can actually do something about your problem, or you're going to leave the house fifteen minutes earlier every morning.

2. *Describe your new behavior in writing*. Not only does this give you a record of what you're doing, but the physical act of writing something down and then reading it back forms the first neurochemical thread of axons in your brain that will eventually form the permanent mental chain called *habit*.

3. *Share it*. Announce the change publicly. Tell the world or at least someone in your support system. Changing habits is never easy and you need all the boosters you can get. (Avoid the "friend" who says, "Aw, come on, cheat a little." If you run across someone this insensitive, reply in an indignant voice, "Why should I cheat myself?")

4. *Act immediately* — or as soon as possible. If you decide you will stop complaining, start *not* complaining tomorrow. Or when you go home at the end of the day, resist the temptation to complain to your spouse, roommate, or children. Act immediately on whatever you have decided.

5. *Don't give up for three weeks*. Maxwell Maltz, the author of *Psychocybernetics*, said that if you move your wastepaper basket to the other side of your desk, you'll throw paper on the floor for the first three weeks. It takes that long to change an ingrained habit. So give yourself enough time to learn a new habit, to remember where you put your wastepaper basket. There's another reason for the three-week

timetable: It's a lot easier to try something different and uncomfortable if you see an end to it, a definite time limit rather than a dreary chore stretching on forever. The "carrot" of reaching the end of those twenty-one days keeps you going. At the end of that time, either your new regime has become a habit or its benefits are so overwhelming that you will be eager to continue it until it *does* become a habit.

The Railroad Tracks of Life

In *Make Your Mind Work for You*, Joan Minninger and Eleanor Dugan say that "Habits are like railroad tracks. You lay them down with a lot of effort so that later you can get where you want to be, smoothly and easily."

Continuing the railroad analogy, you sometimes find that a particular station or spur line is no longer useful. Then it's time to lay new track. "Brains don't learn to get results," says psychologist Richard Bandler, "they learn to go in directions." What direction do you want your tracks to go in? Surely planning your life is as important as planning a railroad route.

Minninger and Dugan describe a technique for getting different parts of the mind to agree to develop or change a habit. According to the authors, "Orders from our mental executive are like New Year's resolutions. These are *oughts* (musts) that quickly turn into *oughts* (zeros) because they have no support from the other parts of the mind." Minninger and Dugan recommend a total-mind approach, dividing the mind into five parts: the executive and four responding minds, the Wondering, Organizing, Reacting, and Knowing parts (creating the acronym WORK). For changing habits, the routine is:

Assess the situation (Knowing part)

Evaluate any conflicts (Reacting part)

Come up with structures (Organizing part)

Provide energy for the task (Wondering part)

Make Your Mind Work for You advocates using playful techniques rather than self-harassment to overcome resistance when you decide to change a habit. For instance, you can tell yourself that "every time I write an appointment or phone number directly in my book instead of on the back of an old envelope, I'll draw a little silly face next to it."

Even if you choose not to draw the comic face, you have begun the change you want to make.

It took a lot of strength to create the habits that you have now. They represent your personal power. You can use that same power to go somewhere else. Like using jujitsu, you can learn to leverage yourself to where you want to be.

A Sure Sign of Commitment

Alan Cimberg, a top sales trainer for thirty-five years, got his first sales job selling encyclopedias door to door one summer. "That's the best selling of all," he says. "I think if a man walked in and said he had experience selling house to house, I would hire him on the spot. Do you know why? Because the house-to-house salesman is committed. That's the formula: What he was, he will be."

Even if you didn't have that kind of commitment in the past, you can develop it now. What you are, you will be.

YOUR ASSIGNMENT:
Choosing Habits

"The reason worry kills more people than work is that more people worry than work."

Robert Frost

Habits I have that help me:

_____

Habits I have that don't help me:

_____

Habits I want to acquire:

_____

Habits I want to get rid of:

_____

Here are some areas of my life where habit plays a major role. How do I evaluate myself?

My appearance

What I like:

_____

What I want to improve:

_____

What I'm going to do:

_____

When I'm going to start:

_____

My personality

What I like:

_____

What I want to improve:

_____

What I'm going to do:

_____

When I'm going to start:

_____

My relationships with mate and friends

What I like:

_____

What I want to improve:

_____

What I'm going to do:

_____

When I'm going to start:

_____

My personal development

What I like:

_____

What I want to improve:

_____

What I'm going to do:

_____

When I'm going to start:

_____

My work

What I like:

_____

What I want to improve:

_____

What I'm going to do:

_____

When I'm going to start:

_____

CHAPTER 14

Time Management

> *"Tomorrow, and tomorrow,*
> *and tomorrow creeps in this*
> *petty pace from day to day,*
> *to the last syllable of*
> *recorded time..."*
>
> Shakespeare, *Macbeth*
>
> *"Kill time and you kill your career."*
>
> B. C. Forbes

Your future is the only time you have left. If you want to take charge of your life, you have to take charge of your time. You are no more exempt from time's inexorable passing than Macbeth. Whether time is your friend or foe depends on how you use it.

Clichés That Work

The problem with clichés is that, although they often contain momentous truths, they become almost meaningless with repetition. You probably hear information every day that could turn your life around, but you ignore it simply because you've heard it so many times before and it has never made any difference in your life. Fortunately, sometimes something "clicks" and the cliché changes our lives forever.

Some years back Realtor Bob Jansen told an audience, "If you practiced playing the violin in your spare time, one day you could play in a symphony orchestra." Now that is definitely a cliché, something that you have heard many times in many forms, but Bob is living proof that it works. One day, he decided to follow his own advice and actually do it. For five years he practiced the violin in his spare time and, believe it or not, he got to play in an orchestra. Twenty years later, he's still playing with them.

Spending Time Like Money

Too many people spend their time as they spend their money — they go for every bright trinket they come upon so there is nothing left for the important things. The average American family spends approximately seven hours a day watching television. Now, there are some wonderful television programs, but we need to make conscious choices about what we are going to watch, and turn off the set when they are over. Don't be a couch potato. Ask yourself: Is this program improving me as a person? Enriching me? (Don't forget that relaxation counts as enrichment and a few minutes of laughing at Bugs Bunny may equal lengthier, more expensive therapy.) Is this program helping me toward my goals? Is there anything else I would rather be doing right now?

No Time for Planning

Alex MacKenzie, a time management expert, queried five hundred executives about their use of time. Incredibly, 83 percent replied that they didn't have time to keep up with the reading in their field and 72 percent said they didn't have time to plan! When managers don't plan or keep up with their fields, MacKenzie points out, consequences can be disastrous.

Some people feel that planning requires rigid scheduling with no room for experiments, side trips, or pleasure. In *Make Your Mind Work for You*, Joan Minninger and Eleanor Dugan compare nonplanners to jellyfish: "People who have no plans are like jellyfish, drifting back and forth between existence in the water and extinction on the shore. Farther out in the ocean are the whales and dolphins, cavorting, playing, enjoying themselves immensely, but always following their migration patterns, their *plans*. Is the life-plan of a whale really more restrictive than the drifting of a jellyfish?"

How to Create Time

One hour a day every day adds up to nine 40-hour weeks each year. Most of us use the excuse that we don't have time to read, exercise, or be with our families. But if we got up half an hour earlier every day, we would "create" four-and-a-half working weeks a year. Eliminating just fifteen wasted minutes each day gives you more than eleven extra days each year. Good time management techniques create extra time in which to achieve your goals.

Many people say that time is money. That is true to a certain extent, with one important difference. You can put money in the bank and draw the money itself back out plus interest. But once you've invested an hour, the hour itself is gone. All you have is the interest. (This is the real lesson of Macbeth's realization.) This interest, however, is what life is all about. When you spend time on training, learning, developing yourself, you get it back many times over.

Efficiency and Effectiveness

Don't confuse activity with accomplishment. Choose the best ways to use your time instead of racing around in a circle. Management expert Peter Drucker sees a big difference between being efficient and being effective.

☆ Efficiency is doing things right.

☆ Effectiveness is doing the right things.

There are two reasons why people don't manage their time well. Either they have not been taught proper techniques or they are not motivated. For example, people often say, "I'm going to wait until I have more time to get organized" or "Time management doesn't work for me. I always lose my list." If you offer excuses like these, then your problem is motivation.

The ABC's of To Do Lists

Every time you think of something you need or want to do, write it down. At your daily organizing session, these notes become your To Do List for the next day, the next week, the next year.

Now take your To Do List for tomorrow and turn it into an ABC List. You should be able to divide everything you want to do into three categories:

The A's: major aspects of your job, business, or personal life

The B's: not as urgent

The C's: bothersome but they must be done eventually

Each day I take my To Do List and code it with A's, B's, and C's. This helps me make sure that I don't spend all of my time with the smaller, time-consuming C jobs when I should be working toward A goals. Your ABC To Do List can be the most useful tool you have at your disposal.

Jot down everything you'd *like* to do or *have* to do the next day. Of course, you rarely think of things in their order of importance. That's why you go back and decide which things are most important, have the highest payoff, bring you closer to your goals — the things that are going to make you happy and successful — and put a big A next to those items. These are the items you should do first.

Write a B next to the things that are important, but are not high-priority.

Then anything that is nice if you get around to doing it becomes a C priority item. Do not do C items first thing in the morning when you are energetic.

First thing in the morning you should do the "icky" things — the priorities that you're not crazy about. Otherwise you will allow your other work to expand throughout the day, and at six o'clock you'll be able to yawn and say, "What a hard worker I am. Too bad I didn't get around to calling that unhappy customer."

When you complete an item on your schedule, cross it out. That makes you feel good. And keep the sheets of your ABCs To Do pad pinned to your calendar so that your weekly and monthly schedules are also with your ABC pad. Before the end of each day, plan the next day.

Periodically recheck your checklists. Time management expert John Lee suggests that we do "after action" analyses of everything we do. At the end of the day or after a major activity, check to see whether you have left anything important off your To Do List. Decide how you can prepare better next time.

Planning Ahead

At the end of each week, take your calendar and plan the following week. I plan out the next week *and* month in advance at the same sitting. Everything I need to know about speaking engagements or travel plans or appointments is written in four weeks ahead.

If you like, you can have separate To-Do pads for each day of the week — Monday, Tuesday, and so forth, and jot down things as you think of them. Then consolidate these lists onto your weekly list.

People tell me that they have problems with losing lists, not keeping them up, and starting projects without finishing them. If that happens to you, perhaps you are being unrealistic with your schedule. Do not write eight pages of To Do items for Monday. That's far too many. You shouldn't be working with more than two pages. To Do pads are like goals: If you plan them too big, they don't work. If you schedule too much for yourself, the same thing happens.

Many people say that their high-priority items involve such big projects that they never get around to doing them. If this happens to you, find an hour of peace and quiet to think, plan, organize, and do. Sometimes that may seem impossible, but one uninterrupted hour is the equivalent of at least three hours with interruptions. (Even four 15-minute segments are far less effective than that one solid hour.)

Logging Your Time

Try this time management exercise. Fill out the following time logs for your "Average Working Day" and your "Ideal Working Day." Start with what happens on an average day. Block out time for each activity you ordinarily do. The logs starts at 5:00 A.M. If you don't get up until 7:30, put a big X in the blocks from 5:00 until 7:30. Don't list each detail of what you do, just the major activities in a typical workday.

AVERAGE WORKING DAY – TIME LOG

A.M.	5:00-5:30	‖
	5:30-6:00	‖
	6:00-6:30	‖
	6:30-7:00	‖
	7:00-7:30	‖
	7:30-8:00	‖
	8:00-8:30	‖
	8:30-9:00	‖
	9:00-9:30	‖
	9:30-10:00	‖
	10:00-10:30	‖
	10:30-11:00	‖
	11:00-11:30	‖
	11:30-Noon	‖
P.M.	Noon-12:30	‖
	12:30-1:00	‖
	1:00-1:30	‖
	1:30-2:00	‖
	2:00-2:30	‖
	2:30-3:00	‖
	3:00-3:30	‖

3:30-4:00	‖
4:00-4:30	‖
4:30-5:00	‖
5:00-5:30	‖
5:30-6:00	‖
6:00-6:30	‖
6:30-7:00	‖
7:00-7:30	‖
7:30-8:00	‖
8:00-8:30	‖
8:30-9:00	‖
9:00-9:30	‖
9:30-10:00	‖
10:00-10:30	‖
10:30-11:00	‖
11:00-11:30	‖
11:30-MIDNT	‖

A.M.

MIDNT-12:30	‖
12:30-1:00	‖
1:00-1:30	‖
1:30-2:00	‖

Don't Overbook

Did you write in an activity for every single space during your waking hours? That's unrealistic! Make plans that allow time for unexpected emergencies. Time management techniques often fail because the people using them are unrealistic. They schedule every minute of their time; consequently, the first time an emergency comes along they get flustered, or they think these techniques don't work. Be realistic in your planning.

Book Blocks of Time

Many executives find that using a time log helps them reserve larger blocks of time for projects that can't be picked up and put down easily. Even if you have an open-door policy, this is essential for high-priority items. Schedule yourself for at least one uninterrupted hour a day. Early in the morning is good — at home before the family gets up or at the office before anyone else arrives — but some people prefer lunchtime at the office, before dinner, or late at night after everyone is in bed.

Your Ideal Day

Now imagine an ideal workday. Would you get up an hour earlier? Would you schedule something before beginning work (exercise, meditation, socializing, planning)? Would you set aside time during the day for phone calls, for errands like going to the bank and post office? For personal relationships? For reading? For watching television or listening to music? Your life will never be perfect, but unless you have a vision of perfection, you don't know what to work toward.

IDEAL WORKING DAY – TIME LOG

A.M.	5:00-5:30	‖
	5:30-6:00	‖
	6:00-6:30	‖
	6:30-7:00	‖
	7:00-7:30	‖
	7:30-8:00	‖
	8:00-8:30	‖
	8:30-9:00	‖
	9:00-9:30	‖
	9:30-10:00	‖
	10:00-10:30	‖
	10:30-11:00	‖
	11:00-11:30	‖
	11:30-Noon	‖
P.M.	Noon-12:30	‖
	12:30-1:00	‖
	1:00-1:30	‖
	1:30-2:00	‖
	2:00-2:30	‖
	2:30-3:00	‖
	3:00-3:30	‖

3:30-4:00	‖
4:00-4:30	‖
4:30-5:00	‖
5:00-5:30	‖
5:30-6:00	‖
6:00-6:30	‖
6:30-7:00	‖
7:00-7:30	‖
7:30-8:00	‖
8:00-8:30	‖
8:30-9:00	‖
9:00-9:30	‖
9:30-10:00	‖
10:00-10:30	‖
10:30-11:00	‖
11:00-11:30	‖
11:30-MIDNT	‖
A.M. MIDNT-12:30	‖
12:30-1:00	‖
1:00-1:30	‖
1:30-2:00	‖

Your "Ideal Working Day" is your model for the future. How can you turn it into a reality?

Start by applying the following time blasters.

Decide What's Important

Discover what is vital and what is trivial. This is known as the 80-20 rule: 80 percent of the value is accounted for by 20 percent of the items, while 20 percent of the value is accounted for by 80 percent of the items. Learn to concentrate on the high-value "20 percent" items.

Estimate how much of your time a project is worth. One day I walked into my hairstyling salon (I also had an office there) and found my administrative assistant folding towels. I said, "How much do you think folding towels is worth per hour compared to organizing my schedule and booking speaking engagements?" If you make $10,000 a year, your time is worth $5 an hour, based on the forty- hour week. When you make $50,000, your time is worth $25 an hour. If someone making $5 an hour can do a task 80 percent as effectively as someone making $25 an hour, maybe he should do it.

Make the best use of your time. Give the right kind of time — the high-energy time — to the important tasks, your A projects.

Know What You Shouldn't Do

When I wrote the first edition of *Get What You Want*, my staff wanted a party to celebrate the book. (Frankly, they liked any excuse to celebrate anything.) I said, "Fine, if we have a party, will you do all the work? Will you decorate the hall, hang up the streamers, blow up the balloons, invite the people, chop up the cheese, pour out the wine, and clean up after it?" "Yes, Patricia!"

Now, my staff was very much like some of the people you work with — once the enthusiasm wears off, they're not so excited — so again I confirmed. I said, "Are you absolutely sure that when the novelty has worn off you will still want to do all the work, hang up the streamers, blow up the balloons, and so forth?" Again, the affirmative. Two days before the party, I was walking out of the salon through a big hall out- side our business that we were allowed to use for parties. My favorite employee was up at the top of the stepladder, blowing up balloons, and I knew that she would be there until probably nine o'clock that night.

I thought I should stay to help her — teamwork and all that! But, fortunately, in a moment of insight one of my own speeches came to mind:

There is no point doing well what
you shouldn't be doing at all.

My job had been to write the book. My job had been to negotiate with the publisher. My job had been to think of ways to sell the book. My job was *not* to blow up balloons. And I had had their agreement and commitment to do the work. Even though my friends tease me (I have a lot of hot air they say, and could have been the best balloon-blower-upper in Northern California), I left to work on the projects that only I could do for our business.

Define the Problem

Some years ago, the *Harvard Business Review* compared the work styles of Japanese and American businessmen. They reported that the Japanese spent much longer clarifying a problem than their American counterparts. With this approach, the solution often became obvious. American businessmen, on the other hand, spent more time thinking directly about the solution. This direct approach fits the direct American personality, but sometimes the problem had not been clearly thought out or clearly stated. The solution then was worthless. Clarify what you want to accomplish. A problem well stated is a problem half-solved.

Make Meetings Work for You

Meetings are one of the biggest time wasters in business. Nobody benefits from poorly run meetings. Always schedule your meetings in a cluster. If they are stretched out through the day or week, you will do little but mark time between them. Having them scheduled back-to-back with brief time buffers between motivates others to use you well during your time with them. It also sets a deadline and gets you out of those endless tail-chasing or finger-pointing sessions that pass for communication in some organizations.

1. *Start on time*. The moment people assume that meetings will start late, they'll gradually show up later and later.

2. *Have an agenda*, and a set time frame. If it's going to be a short meeting, stand up. Don't let people get comfortable.

3. *Have a time limit*. Schedule meetings at the end of the day or before lunch when people will want to leave.

4. *Call on experts*. Learn to use the intelligence and knowledge of other people. Only fools pretend they already know everything.

The Swiss Cheese Technique

Time management expert Alan Lakein says we should attack big projects and turn them into Swiss cheese by taking lots of bite-size pieces out of them. For example, some people leave their receipts unsorted until they sit down to do their taxes on April 15. The mountain of paper is just too overwhelming. One approach is to log all your deductibles into a ledger once a month when you pay bills. Another is to sort and tally receipts whenever you have spare time. While you are waiting on the phone, put your gasoline receipts in a separate pile. When you find twenty minutes, sort through your lunch vouchers. If you cut large projects up into smaller sections, the big chores suddenly aren't so overwhelming.

Several years ago I had my house decorated. Displaced items from all over the house made their way to my desktop, until it was piled high and I couldn't concentrate on current projects. I took everything off the desk and put the items in the bottom of my filing cabinet. Then, whenever I had twenty minutes or half an hour, I'd open the drawer, take something out, put it where it belonged, and close the drawer. My desk stayed tidy, projects were completed, and I wasn't overwhelmed. (If you try this, be *sure* you have the discipline to attack that drawer. Don't acquire the habit of "organizing" by sweeping everything into a hiding place and then ignoring the items until they no longer matter.)

Don't Be Perfect

Murray Raphel is a direct mail specialist in Atlantic City. He's also a top retailer. Whenever he is asked for an order or opinion, he immediately turns to his typewriter and taps it out. Someone once called him and criticized his spelling and typing. Murray asked, "Did you understand what the note said?" Yes, the complainer replied. "How long do you plan to keep my note?" Murray asked. "I've already done what you suggested and thrown it away," the man replied. Murray's point: "Some things have to be done perfectly. Some things don't."

Avoid striving for perfection on things that don't matter. There are many things that we don't have to do perfectly. Balancing a checkbook, perhaps, but sharpening pencils, you don't. Remember that people are paid to get results, not to be perfect.

And don't waste your time on regrets. Trying to rewrite history is futile. Don't spend time rehashing former decisions, justifying bad ones, or salvaging poor time investments that ought to be written off. Use the past as a guide for the future, not as an excuse for not dealing with it.

Do It Now

Don't procrastinate. The great eighteenth-century English literary light Samuel Johnson once said, "Procrastination is the thief of time." One of the biggest reasons that people are unsuccessful is because they wait to do something until it doesn't matter any more—in which case, they've lost more than just time. They have surrendered control of their lives to others or to random chance.

Indecision is often a form of procrastination. There is a time for deliberation and a time for action. The well-known prayer might be altered to "Lord, give me the patience to wait for the right moment, the energy to act decisively, and the wisdom to know when to do which."

Take Control of the Telephone

We can't live *with* them and we can't live *without* them. Telephones are the indispensable monsters of modern society. Take charge of your phone. Devise a way to get off before you get on. Say things like, "I just have two minutes; this is why I called."

Don't automatically ask, "How are you?" People will either automatically reply "fine" or—if they've just gotten divorced, fallen in love, or been ill—take twenty minutes of your day to tell you how they really are. Express your personal interest in people in other ways. When you open every phone conversation with several minutes of social positioning, you stand a good chance of not getting to the point of your call before your listener is summoned away. When someone asks me, "How are you?" and I know it's just a preprogrammed conversation opener, I usually answer, "Busy—tell me, what can I do for you?" If they say, "Can I ask you a question?" I reply, "You can ask me two as long as I can answer them in two minutes." Both answers indicate a genuine concern in the other person's business, but free me of time-wasting preparatory chat. In business, efficiency can be better manners than insincere, ritualistic exchanges.

Before you pick up the phone, make a written outline of the topics you want to discuss. This will save calling back.

If your business requires you to call people, make your telephone calls early in the morning. Then, the people you're calling are more likely to be in their offices and at their best. People often get irritated as the day goes on. If you're in a job where you are soliciting appointments or business by telephone, it is better to call people early, before they get bogged down.

Time Savers at Work

☆ Go to work before (or after) the rush hours. Beat the traffic.

☆ When you go to a parking garage, don't drive around the lower levels searching for a spot; drive straight to the top, where you know you can park.

☆ In small buildings, don't wait for elevators; walk.

☆ Take a meditation break rather than a coffee break.

☆ Handle paperwork only once. Every time you pick up a piece of paper, rip off the corner. If you pick it up a second time and you haven't finished with it, rip another corner. If you pick it up again and still don't do anything with it, rip another corner. This way, if you keep picking it up, eventually your problem is eliminated.

☆ Keep all your papers, notes, and plans in one place.

☆ Get somebody else to scan magazines and rip out articles that may be of interest to you, or do so yourself and read them on an airplane or while waiting for appointments. Consider subscribing to a clipping service if you want to keep on top of a special field.

☆ Use a calendar system that works for you. In her time management seminar, Dru Scott suggests you buy yourself a nice leather folder with your name embossed on it—something so beautiful you won't lose it.

☆ Confirm, don't assume. Planes get canceled, people forget, messages get garbled, important papers slip behind filing cabinets. Save yourself hours by taking a minute to confirm. Don't assume that because you made an appointment with someone, that person is going to be there. Confirm before you leave. Don't assume the plane is on time. Call the airport. Don't assume that everyone will know exactly what to do for an important event. Confirm, confirm, confirm.

☆ Learn from other people's experience. Don't reinvent the wheel. Consult people, books, and organizations that can help you.

☆ Do several things at once *when it is appropriate*. (Listen to informational tapes while you're driving a car, riding on an airplane, having a manicure, or waiting in line for a movie. Have a shoulder rest on your telephone so you can write checks and open mail while being kept on "hold." At home, put on nail polish, exercise, and watch TV all at once.)

Handling Mail

☆ When you're sorting your mail, put your fun mail (notes from friends) in a bag to open when you have time to sit with your feet up.

☆ Learn to sift rapidly through junk mail for the few items of interest. (But be careful — credit cards are often sent in boring envelopes to confuse thieves.)

☆ Answer mail by recycling letters. It's quite acceptable to write notations on the letters you receive and send them back. Make a photocopy if you want one for your file.

Handling People

☆ Always go to the office of the person you want to talk to. It's a lot easier to get out of somebody else's office than to push them out of yours. And don't allow long-winded visitors to sit in your office. Keep them standing.

☆ Whenever you plan to meet someone, especially someone in the habit of arriving late, be sure to meet him or her in a place where you can accomplish something while you're waiting.

☆ If a salesperson wants to talk to you, say, "I'll give you twenty minutes — if you want to come and talk to me while I eat my lunch." (This worked for me when I had a salon, although it's not so appropriate now.) When you agree to hear a sales presentation, you have a right to limit the time.

Managing at Home

☆ Make blender meals. Protein powder, fruit, and milk or fruit juice mixed in a blender is very filling, very nutritious, and saves time.

☆ Use your freezer as a time management device. I make large batches of vegetable casseroles and soup and freeze them. They provide quick, hearty meals for many weeks for me and my staff.

☆ Eat out. This especially saves time in restaurants you visit frequently (unless you use dinner out as a time to relax). Then you don't even have to look at the menu. When your food is brought to you, ask for the check.

☆ If you can, pay other people to do things for you — to shop, clean your house, or do your gardening.

☆ Meet with your friends in groups rather than individually. Breakfast is good.

☆ Make sure you have a spare of any appliance you use frequently. Then if it breaks you don't go crazy.

☆ Do your shopping by phone or computer.

☆ Buy in quantity. My father's philosophy was "if you want ten, buy a hundred wholesale." As a time management technique, I buy thirty birthday cards at a time, ten tubes of toothpaste. It cuts down shopping time.

Personal Time Savers

☆ Make appointments with yourself. For me, it's important to spend at least fifteen minutes soaking in a bubblebath now and then. (I think that this comforting diversion should be on everyone's schedule, for his or her peace of mind.)

☆ For women: Consider wearing your hair short, unless you're prepared to invest a lot of time in maintaining it long. (Or wearing it long enough to twist up with pins, avoiding time with hot rollers and styling brushes.)

☆ Have a wardrobe consultant or someone else whose taste you trust preview clothes for you. This way you go straight to the store and try on the possibles instead of spending hours or days sifting through racks.

☆ Learn how to cope with unwanted invitations. In 1979, the *San Francisco Chronicle* published an article about how people decline invitations. One woman interviewed said, "Thank you, but my husband hates social gatherings." Playwright Anita Loos wished she had the integrity to respond the way a friend of hers did. That friend simply writes, "Mr. John Golden sincerely regrets that he has no desire to accept your kind invitation." Businesswoman Ellen Newman favored more tactful honesty. If it's a free night, she tells people that she and her husband "need that time very badly for ourselves."

☆ Start your Christmas shopping in January. Once a month write all your birthday cards and put Post-its on with what day you need to post them, or jot "Mail Sam's birthday card" on your calendar. Have a dozen clever gifts tucked away that are appropriate for anybody.

☆ Know when you are at your best and most energetic. For most people, that's in the morning. Plan to be doing the most important things when *you're in top form.*

☆ Try to eliminate one time waster from your life each week.

Three Coping Styles

Life has never been simple, and each generation is always sure that the decisions and choices they face each day are harder than ever before in history. We do have many more options, but instead of making things easier, this multiplicity of choices can be stressful, even immobilizing. It's like facing the world's biggest smorgasbord table and not knowing where to start.

Three ways of dealing with the multiple demands of today — personal, job, home, community — have emerged in the 1980s.

1. *Limiting*. Avoiding conflicts by focusing totally on one area, usually career. Efficient but restrictive.

2. *Staggering*. Devoting time blocks alternately to different demands: "This year I'll concentrate on making vice president, next year I'll get my body in shape, the year after that I'll go back to school and maybe get married."

3. *Juggling*. Participating in all important areas at once, juggling the time and energy demands on an as-needed basis.

Juggling has some distinct benefits — you get to try all the goodies on the table at once — but juggling is also the most difficult. "Jugglers" need strong support systems, both within their families and in the community.

According to Dr. Rela Geffen Monson, who conducted a 1985 study of one thousand high-level professional and career women, American women have a strong tendency to cope by *limiting* — avoiding conflict with careers by not marrying, or by marrying but not having children. Interestingly, however, two-thirds of the Jewish women who took part in the study were married and most had children. "The majority of [these] respondents saw some positive connection between their commitment to . . . the Jewish community and their professional lives."

Helpful mates were cited as the biggest contributors to successful juggling. Financial security was also important; about half the households had annual incomes over $65,000 and 16 percent had incomes over $150,000.

How you choose to cope is a matter of personal style, personal resources, and what you are up against. But remember Auntie Mame's famous observation: "Life is a banquet and most poor sons of bitches are starving!"

YOUR ASSIGNMENT:
Budgeting My Time

"The cost of a thing is the amount of what I will call life which is required to be exchanged for it, immediately or in the long run."

Henry David Thoreau

	Always	Usually	Sometimes	Never
1. Do I know what my major goals are?	[ ]	[ ]	[ ]	[ ]
2. Do I know what I want to eliminate from my life?	[ ]	[ ]	[ ]	[ ]
3. Am I realistic about where my time goes?	[ ]	[ ]	[ ]	[ ]
4. Am I aware of my biggest time wasters?	[ ]	[ ]	[ ]	[ ]
5. Could I get up an hour earlier?	[ ]	[ ]	[ ]	[ ]
6. Is it possible to have an hour of uninterrupted time?	[ ]	[ ]	[ ]	[ ]

	Always	Usually	Sometimes	Never
7. Do I know how to get off the telephone before I get on?	[ ]	[ ]	[ ]	[ ]
8. Do I make lists?	[ ]	[ ]	[ ]	[ ]
9. Do I have a tidy desk?	[ ]	[ ]	[ ]	[ ]
10. Do I find time for self-improvement?	[ ]	[ ]	[ ]	[ ]
11. Do I find time to exercise?	[ ]	[ ]	[ ]	[ ]
12. Do I find time for the special people in my life?	[ ]	[ ]	[ ]	[ ]
13. If I had an extra hour a day, would I know how to use it?	[ ]	[ ]	[ ]	[ ]
14. Do I say "no" often enough?	[ ]	[ ]	[ ]	[ ]
15. Do I have a clearly defined written list of objectives?	[ ]	[ ]	[ ]	[ ]
16. Do I assign each objective a priority, **in writing**?	[ ]	[ ]	[ ]	[ ]

	Always	Usually	Sometimes	Never
17. Do I plan and schedule my time on a weekly as well as on a daily basis?	[ ]	[ ]	[ ]	[ ]
18. Do I use travel and waiting time productively?	[ ]	[ ]	[ ]	[ ]
19. Do I delegate as much work and responsibility as I can?	[ ]	[ ]	[ ]	[ ]
20. Do I utilize my assistants and secretary as well as I can?	[ ]	[ ]	[ ]	[ ]
21. Do I take time each day to sit back and think about what I am doing and what I am trying to accomplish?	[ ]	[ ]	[ ]	[ ]
22. Have I eliminated one time waster during the past week?	[ ]	[ ]	[ ]	[ ]
23. Do I feel in control of my time and on top of my job?	[ ]	[ ]	[ ]	[ ]
24. Am I productive in meetings?	[ ]	[ ]	[ ]	[ ]

	Always	Usually	Sometimes	Never
25. Do I procrastinate?	[ ]	[ ]	[ ]	[ ]
26. Do I resist the temptation to get involved in other people's activities?	[ ]	[ ]	[ ]	[ ]
27. Do I control my schedule so that other people do not waste their time waiting for me?	[ ]	[ ]	[ ]	[ ]
28. Do I resist doing things for others that they probably could and should do for themselves?	[ ]	[ ]	[ ]	[ ]
29. Do I accumulate unnecessary paperwork?	[ ]	[ ]	[ ]	[ ]
30. Do I effectively control interruptions and drop-in visitors rather than allowing them to control me?	[ ]	[ ]	[ ]	[ ]
31. Am I better organized than I was six months ago?	[ ]	[ ]	[ ]	[ ]
32. Do I see the need for improvement in the next six months?	[ ]	[ ]	[ ]	[ ]

CHAPTER 15

Twelve Tips for Turning Potential into Performance

> *"Success comes in cans—*
> *not cannots."*

Joel Weldon

Here are the twelve keys for turning your potential into positive action.

1. Understand which things deserve your energy.

With so many fascinating opportunities before you each day, how do you decide which are for you? My brother, Robert, has formulated four questions for judging whether an action is appropriate for him.

- ☆ *Does this earn a living for me?* In a material world, we all have responsibilities that cannot be ignored.
- ☆ *Can I learn from this?* Can I grow as a human being by doing this particular piece of work?
- ☆ *Can I have fun?* If I can't have fun doing whatever I'm doing, if I can't enjoy it, then it's really not worth doing; if life is only drudgery, it's hardly worth living.
- ☆ *Is it useful?* Sooner or later any piece of useful work will involve us with other people. Will this action bring me together with people in a worthwhile way?

These, Robert explains, are his four criteria. "When I confront something," he says, "these are the things I use to measure the chances for a positive outcome for me."

2. Know the difference between "low-payoff" and "high-payoff" activities.

When you invest your time, you want to invest it in high-return projects. The lists below provide a profile of the activities with the potential for the highest return.

Characteristics of low-payoff activities	Characteristics of high-payoff activities
Not related to goal	Directly related to goal
Comfortable to do	Might not be pleasant
No risk involved	Tend to involve risk
Routine	Might be difficult
Noncreative, anyone can do it	Can't be delegated
Trivial	Important

Investing your time and energy is like investing your money. You may risk it and lose it. But risk is what spells the difference between getting what you want and sitting on the sidelines.

3. Clean out the closets of your life.

Have you ever looked at the clothes in your closet with a critical eye: the bargain shoes in the wrong color; the expensive suit you got on sale that never fit; the "great" shirt that was a gift from someone you love?

I had all of those items in my closet. Then a wardrobe consultant friend came over and made me clean out the clothes that didn't fit or that no longer represented my self-image. It was an exhilarating feeling. Now the clothes I wear make me feel and look great, and project the image I like.

Your clothes closet isn't the only hiding place for negative things in your life. You have a self-image closet too. Take a serious look at what you find there. Try cleaning it out. Throw out ideas that no longer fit your lifestyle or your experiences.

Clean your closet of certain old friends as well—the ones who have become acquaintances. Too often we spend our energies with people whose interests have grown apart from ours.

Clean the negative people out of your life's closet. Some folks cannot accept your achievements, insisting it's only "a fluke" when you finally attain a great goal. Their own insecurities require them to shoot other people down. It is time to let them know you are proud of your achievements, and then move on to someone who will support you in your endeavors.

Closets may be hiding places for our outmoded clothes and ideas, but they are also where we store the building blocks for our daily lives. Don't let them get cluttered with outdated ideas.

4. Keep the sand out of the pastry of your life.

Imagine someone baking a chocolate cake. In addition to flour, sugar, and salt, he adds a small spoonful of gritty sand to the recipe. The cake batter is stirred, carefully baked, frosted, and decorated with nuts, cherries, and whipped cream. It looks perfect. At dinner, when you see that cake, what would you do? I would probably cut the biggest slice possible — without appearing to be too greedy — and take a mouthful. My first reaction would be "ummmmm." Then I would notice the sand, push my plate away, and say, "Thanks, it's a beautiful cake — except for the sand."

In the same way, it takes only a small spoonful of negative attitudes or remarks to ruin an otherwise perfect day: colleagues who greet you at work in the morning by complaining about what has already gone wrong; relatives who just smile politely when you tell them about a big raise, a promotion, or an exciting event; people who respond to everything you do with a horror story about someone else who did the same thing with disastrous consequences. These people are the grit in your life. The funny thing is that it doesn't matter whether a friend or a stranger puts the abrasive element in your day — the effect is the same.

Of course, you may be related to the people who specialize in ruining your cake. You can't un-relate yourself from these people, but you can make them aware of what they are doing. Approach Uncle Charley when he is in a good mood and tell the story about the gritty cake. Then the next time he reacts negatively to good news, say nicely, "Hey, Charley, do you realize you are putting sand in my cake?" Perhaps then he will realize how harsh his negative reactions have been on your spirit. He may also be pleased to know that he matters to you, and that his reactions affect your pleasure.

5. Teach people how you want them to treat you.

Confrontations are often necessary and they can occur in many ways. Once I returned from a visit to England and found I had left my alien registration card safely in my desk here in America. (You're not supposed to re-enter the United States without it.) I got off the plane at three in the morning, and the customs officer insisted that my error would cost $10,000. I refused to be intimidated. I looked at him and said calmly, "Would you like me to go get my card now and bring it back in two hours, or shall I take it to the immigration office in the morning?" Of course, he didn't want to stay late and replied, "By all means, take it to the immigration office tomorrow."

On another occasion, I asked the doorman of a hotel where I was giving a talk whether I could leave my car outside for thirty-five minutes. "Fine, no problem," he said, "just leave the keys."

Thirty-five minutes later I was back. Another man was on duty. The first doorman, it seemed, was on his break. I said, "I need the keys to my car." Several dollars were in my hand to tip the first man for letting me leave my car out front, but this character — all six-feet-two-inches of him — sneered, "Well, you're going to have to wait until he's off his break, aren't you?" I pulled myself up to my full five-feet-one-inch height and replied, "I do not appreciate your attitude. Please get my keys." He did.

Emotional Blackmail

A woman at a seminar asked what she should do when she's going to work in the evening and her two-year-old says, "Mommy, I hate you because you're going out." I turned to the audience for answers. One woman stood up and said, "You are allowing yourself to be emotionally blackmailed." Another woman said, "I get the same thing, and I smile and hug her and say, 'I'm going to miss you too, honey. I'll be back as soon as I can.' It's up to *you* whether you interpret your child's fears as blackmail or not."

Another woman came up to me at the break because she did not want to share her thoughts with the group. She said, "If I can make my mentally retarded two-year-old daughter understand that mommy is going out to make money to help buy her 'pretties,' I think somebody should certainly be able to make a normal child understand."

Blackmail is a contract between two people. It only works when both agree to play. We should not accept emotional blackmail from others, just as we should not try to blackmail them. My wonderful friend Karen Trunnelle Dyer, who spent countless hours typing the original manuscript for this book, has children who would sometimes make noise and demand her attention when she was hard at work. She would explain to them, "I am doing this to make more money for all of us. You can help me by playing peacefully near me but not interrupting."

"They learn," Karen told me, "that kisses and catastrophes are more important than money and I can always be interrupted for them, but pointless interruptions will result in fewer treats. When they can feel that they are contributing by cooperating and sharing in the results, they are more willing to keep the interruptions to a minimum."

Often society provides women with only a vague line between good manners and being taken advantage of, between being a caring, nurturing person and being a victim. It's up to the woman to make the line clear and strong, both for herself and others. Joann, the wife of a speaker friend, was formerly married to a man who treated her shabbily. Finally, she thought to herself: If I were being treated this way by a man courting me, I wouldn't dream of marrying him. In a matter of days, she had filed for divorce. She has never regretted that decision.

To teach people how we want to be treated, we must sometimes use a little muscle, refuse to be intimidated. We need to know that we deserve good treatment. If we don't respect ourselves, who will?

6. Develop your speaking skills.

Even though you don't want to be a professional speaker, there is no greater confidence booster in the world than being able to speak comfortably in front of others. According to *The Book of Lists*, people fear speaking in public more than anything else.

Visibility is necessary to succeed in almost any business, and people who can speak clearly and eloquently impress others as superior. If you can address a group, that is a big plus. But just having the confidence to discuss your views with others gives you an edge over your competition.

Your personal life can benefit too. If you often come down with foot-in-mouth disease when you try to discuss sensitive issues with family members, learning how to "do a presentation" — to persuade, offer a plan, express your point of view — can improve personal communications. If you routinely get flustered, angry, or even tearful during intimate discussions, or if you avoid them entirely because of the discomfort, consider developing your speaking skills. (In the old days, *Debating* was part of every school's curriculum, an important lesson of how it is possible to argue on different sides of an issue without losing one's temper or respect for one's opponent.)

Everyone has knowledge and experience to share. If you clam up with nerves in a PTA meeting, a church group, or a staff meeting, you are not sharing your knowledge with other people or contributing to the group decision process.

In 1959, Joel Weldon ("Success comes in cans—not cannots") graduated from high school in what he calls the half of the class that made the top half possible. He was quiet and shy. He studied building construction for two years and worked in various construction jobs until he was twenty-five. He was highly paid, but he had little confidence.

Then the construction industry had one of its regular set-backs. In 1967 Joel went to work selling—or trying to sell—the *World Book* encyclopedia. After two months in the field, Weldon had set a dubious record: 1,200 sales calls and total earnings of $48. He was ready to give up.

How did he change?

Hoping Joel's attitude would improve, his manager gave him a cassette recording of Earl Nightingale's "Lead the Field," lessons on self-management, goals, and potential. Joel listened—and Joel became a top salesman. The tapes didn't *make* him a top salesman, but the Nightingale philosophy enabled Joel to overcome his shyness and lack of confidence. He had always possessed the skills to do well.

This was the first turning point in his sales career. Later he was promoted to a regional management position. Eventually he was responsible for hiring and training hundreds of salespeople. For more than four years, he averaged a sale a day in addition to his management responsibilities. This outstanding achievement earned him nearly every award the company gave for management sales performance. Things had certainly changed.

Joel's second turning point came when he joined Toastmasters International to improve his communication skills. By 1974, he was one of the top three speakers in the Toastmasters International Speech Contest. Not long after that, he was paid his first professional speaking fee—$25 and a free dinner. The demand for his speaking services increased and, as president of Joel H. Weldon and Associates, he became a full-time professional speaker and seminar leader. Using valuable insights on change and success from his own life, Joel began to help others tap their potential and increase their effectiveness. His was one of the most rapid and dramatic climbs in the speaking and training industry. Today, the demand for his time is only one measure of his success.

What you say and how you say it are unfortunately often inseparable. Presentation can eclipse content. As Nixon said after debating Kennedy, "I didn't realize that how I looked was more important than what I said."

When Reagan debated Carter for the first time, a group of executives were brought together by political consultants to watch the program. They were asked afterward to describe how they felt about issues that had been discussed. One said, "I liked the way Reagan shook hands." Another said, "Carter doesn't appear presidential." Another said, "I liked the way Reagan chided Carter." Their reactions had nothing to do with the important issues before the country and everything to do with communication skills.

Finally, I asked Buck Rodgers, author of *The IBM Way* and *Getting the Most Out of Yourself and Others*, if there was one ingredient that guarantees success. "Yes," he replied, "the self-confidence to speak up, even when your point of view is unpopular."

7. Learn to say "no" when necessary.

You don't need to make any excuses for refusing a business proposal or a social invitation. A simple no (possibly followed by thank you) will do. Often we think we should explain our reasons for our behavior to others as if we are responsible to them for our actions.

How to Say "Yes" by Saying "No"

Unassertive people say "yes" when they really want to say "no" so they won't hurt the feelings of others. Ironically, however, they often cause more ill will in the future. But there is a way to say "yes" at the same time you say "no."

My salon in San Francisco was in the same building as the Chamber of Commerce. Naturally I was a member. One of the executives asked me to run a luncheon once a month for their volunteers. I said, "No. Because of my travel schedule, I won't be there often enough. However, let me tell you what I can do. Once a year I'll give a free talk to rev up your volunteers. That way you use a talent of mine that most of your other members don't have." I was saying "yes" and "no" at the same time: "no" to the original request, but "yes" to supporting the organization.

Debbi Steele, sales manager for several small San Francisco hotels, is exceptionally active in the business community and the hospitality industry. Debbi is a generous woman with her time and knowledge. She was always taking time away from her desk to talk to people who wanted to know about the hotel industry, then working late at night to catch up. I told her about my "no/yes" strategy.

One day when we were running she said, "Fripp, you'll be proud of me. I took your advice. A young woman asked me to have lunch with her so I could tell her about the hotel business. I said "no" to her invitation, but gave her two choices: 1) she could run with me at 6:30 in the morning and we could talk, or 2) she could spend the afternoon in my office, working for me for nothing, stuffing envelopes and answering the phone. We would talk while we were working. The young woman decided on the second choice, and afterward thanked me profusely. She now understood what it was going to be like working in a sales manager's office." Both Debbi Steele and the young woman were winners, and Debbi didn't have to work late to catch up.

Things to Think About Before Saying "Yes"

☆ Do I really want to do what I've been asked to do?

☆ Will I benefit personally from the experience?

☆ Will those closest to me benefit?

☆ Will I ever have the opportunity to do this again?

☆ How much of my time is involved?

☆ Can the job be done quickly or will it involve weeks, months, or a year?

☆ How much help will I have, or do I have full responsibility?

☆ Am I being asked to do this job because I'm right for it or because I usually don't say "no"?

☆ Will my family or friends have to take a back seat while I'm involved?

☆ Will I have to cancel other plans in order to make this new commitment?

If you don't have the right answers to these questions, teach yourself to say "no" — or "yes" by saying "no".

8. Practice sowing and reaping.

The best maxim for achieving success in your job, your relationships, and every other aspect of your life is the universal parable about sowing and reaping. The successes you reap in life are the results of the positive energy and hard work which you have sown in the past — *a past that you can begin forming immediately.*

9. Begin to think of your retirement now.

Even if you are twenty. In *Money and Retirement — How to Plan for Lifetime Financial Security*, authors Robert T. LeClair, Stephan R. Leimberg, and Herbert Chasman estimate that we spend 85,000 hours of our life earning a living and about ten hours planning our retirement.

Milt Eisele, a famous winemaker in Napa, California, has a warning for each of us. "When I was around forty-six or so I had a remarkable experience. I was invited to go to lunch with employees in the Sears Roebuck home office. They were retiring one of their old telephone operators. My host told me about Sears' experiment with counseling their retirees. Ten years prior to your actual retirement, the personnel department called you in. Everyone would shake hands with you and say, 'Ten years from today, we're going to do this for keeps. Now what are you going to do when you retire?' The typical answer was, 'Well, I'm going to go fishing or go hunting, I'm going to travel, I'm going to play golf.'

"So Sears made arrangements to have people prepare for these objectives during this ten-year period. This process made most of them realize that just golf or travel wouldn't fulfill them — and they came to this realization when they still had ten years to plan. That made a lasting impression on me. So did something else.

"About eight years later, a neighbor in Palo Alto retired. He had been president of one of the largest railroads in the country. The company dropped him from the board. Like many other retired executives, he and his wife went to Europe, bought a Mercedes, and toured for six months. When he came home, he suddenly thought, What in the world will I do with myself?

"Since we lived near Stanford University, it seemed appropriate that Stanford would have him lecture at the Business School or in the Department of Economics or Finance. But they didn't. I would see him frequently, particularly on Saturday mornings while I was working in my garden, and we would chat.

"Then he was gone for about three months. I thought he was away traveling or on a cruise.

"One Saturday morning he reappeared. I was startled at his appearance. He had two or three days' growth of beard, his pants were not pressed, and he was wearing bedroom slippers. I was really taken aback. 'My God,' I muttered, 'What's happened to you?'

"'Well, I really wasn't feeling very well,' he explained, 'so they put me in the hospital for a couple of months. They couldn't find anything wrong with me, but I continued to feel lousy and they decided the best thing for me was to return home and be with my wife and friends. You know,' he said after a minute, 'I still feel lousy.'

"Eighteen months later he was dead.

"I don't think he lasted more than five years after his retirement. This said to me that you've got to have some challenges, some feeling of achievement each day. If not, before long, you won't be looking at just the end of the day."

10. Make contracts with yourself — before someone else makes them for you.

A psychiatrist wrote about a woman who wanted to give up smoking but couldn't. He asked her, "Do you really want to?" She said, "Yes."

"Okay," he said, "any time you smoke, you have to give me ten dollars. I'm going to give the money to the charity of my choice. And I'm going to put updated notices in your synagogue of how much money you are giving to this charity." The charity he chose was the Palestinian Liberation Organization, the PLO.

Moral: It's better to write your own contracts.

11. Be positive

How you start out in the morning sets the tone for how the rest of the day will go. The morning is no time for reality. It's too easy to feel pressured as you rush to get ready. You end up nagging others (or yourself) about all the things they forgot to do yesterday and must remember to do today. That's one reason why lists made the night before are invaluable.

Be sure you create a positive atmosphere at home with affirmations of love and support for your dear ones. Continue your positive pattern with everyone you meet. I used to park at a large downtown garage at six o'clock in the morning. When I got there, the nice young men would say, "How are you, Miss Fripp?" I'd say, "Terrific! Marvelous! Great! Never felt so good in all my life." Obviously, that wasn't always true. But people react to you the way you present yourself to them.

After I had parked there a couple of years, one of the young attendants said, "Miss Fripp, you are the only regular that we dare ask, 'How are you?' We have a game to see who gets to you first." My cheerful morning greeting, intended to raise my own spirits, had paid other dividends. Some of those nice young men came to me for haircuts. And don't you think they may have put themselves out to extricate my car in the afternoon crush, for that "nice Miss Fripp who is always so pleased to see us" rather than some miserable old crab who comes in here early in the morning? There are so many people who help your life go smoothly who are not on your payroll.

If it's biologically possible, get an early start. I know there are *morning people* and *night people*, but you know who got the worm. Most people are at their best and most positive in the morning, so take advantage of that positivity by being there to work with them. Get up as early as possible (what I call "rolling out of bed on *your* side"). If you want to start getting up an hour earlier than you have been, don't do it all of a sudden. Work up to it. Start getting up ten or fifteen minutes earlier for a week, then another ten or fifteen minutes earlier the next.

Reward yourself for getting to work early. (I have my first cup of coffee, then go to the gym.) Promise yourself that if you get up an hour earlier and accomplish such-and-such by ten o'clock, you will allow yourself to put your feet up for ten minutes, read a marvelous, informative book (like this one), and have a healthful snack. Set your own rewards into your schedule — and also punish yourself for doing things you should not or for not doing things you should. For example, if you say "yes" to somebody when you want to say "no," penalize yourself by balancing your checkbook *without* a calculator.

12. Find the time to be successful.

Shortly after I opened my hairstyling salon, a friend told me about a terrific organizational seminar. I didn't have the time to go myself, so I sent my assistant. She came back and said, "It was great. But I can't just tell you about it, Patricia. You have to experience this yourself." So I did.

When I had finished the course, I realized that time management was not only exciting, but could free me to accomplish my goals more easily. Managing your time efficiently is truly taking charge of your life. You cannot save time; you can only invest it productively. And if you're not enjoying yourself in the process, chances are your productivity is suffering as well.

We have only three things in our lives that we can budget: our money, our energy, and our time. Time management is actually the simplest of the three. It uses only a few simple techniques. The drawback for some people is that they have to be applied diligently.

Think about how you plan your vacations. Well, let's see, you might say to yourself, Where do I want to go? What do I want to experience during my two weeks off? How much will it cost? What plans must be made and special efforts taken so I can thoroughly enjoy it?

Try preparing for your life and your career the same way you prepare for your time off. Begin by establishing your goals: What do you want most out of your career? Think of where you would like to be in five years' time, and in ten. Think about the personal qualities you would like to develop in yourself. If you have never set goals before, start with small ones: I will read a book every week or I will lose ten pounds. Your goals should be challenging ones (it's no fun rising early every day just to send off payments of your bills), but make sure they are also attainable. Be realistic. Then decide on how you will reach your goals.

The next step is setting priorities. What needs to be done first? What do you need to know to achieve your goals, and who can help you? How much will it cost you — in time, commitment, and effort? How much are you willing to pay? Put your ideas on paper. It will help you commit your energy. Share your plans with supportive people around you, whether on the job or at home. Enlist friends' cooperation. Achieving your goals is then a matter of step-by-step persistence.

As Emerson said, "Know then the world exists for you. . . . What *we* are, that only can *we* see. . . . Build therefore your own world." You'll find that a successful career is almost as easy to plan as your summer vacation — and the rewards will last a lot longer.

YOUR ASSIGNMENT:
Turning Potential into Performance

1. Understand which things deserve your energy.

Some things that I want to give more attention to are:

Some things that I want to give less attention to are:

2. Know the difference between low-payoff and high-payoff activities.

My high-payoff activities are:

My low-payoff activities are:

Which of these low-payoff activities can I discard?

3. Clean out the closets of your life.

I am making the following appointments with myself for spring-cleaning my life:

Date

_____ I will clean out my clothes closets.

_____ I will clean out my work area.

_____ I will sit down with my address book, calendar, and a sheet of paper to analyze which of my personal relationships no longer serve any purpose.

4. Keep the sand out of the pastry of your life. The people who often throw sand in my pastry are:

(I will now tell each of them the sand story, so that the next time they spoil a happy moment, I can remind them gently, "You're throwing sand in my cake.")

5. Teach people how you want them to treat you.

I don't like the way the following people treat me:

My strategy for changing each one's behavior is:

6. Develop your speaking skills.

I rate my current speaking skills as:

To improve them, I am going to:

7. Learn to say "no" when necessary.

Saying "no"   [ ] is   [ ] isn't   a problem for me.

My positive new strategies for saying "no" (or saying "yes" by saying "no") are:

8. Practice sowing and reaping.

Past examples of my sowing are:

My future plans for sowing are:

9. Begin to think of your retirement now.

My finances, when I retire, will consist of:

When retired, I will spend my time doing:

If I become sick or injured and can't work, my plans are to:

10. Make contracts with yourself — before someone else makes them for you.

A contract I want to make is:

A contract I *need* to make is:

11. Be positive.

My mornings   [ ] are great.

[ ] could be better.

[ ] a disaster.

To make them (even) better, I will:

12. Find the time to be successful.

Three things I need to make time for are:

CHAPTER 16

Possibilities

> *"In life, no one is dealt all the aces. You play the hand you have better than the others."*
>
> Arthur Henry Fripp

Do you remember the television commercial in which Angela Lansbury says, "I want a credit card with possibilities"? Your whole life is a shifting prism of opportunities—*your* possibilities. No matter how much energy, persistence, and confidence you focus on your goals, you will miss some of the good stuff if you fail to notice opportunity. Keep yourself constantly open to possibilities.

When I was twelve years old, I didn't know what was going to happen to me, but I promised myself two things: 1) I was going to be glamorous, and 2) I would have an exciting life. To me that meant getting off airplanes with a mink coat over my shoulder, just like the movie stars. While my friends wanted to marry millionaires, I knew I'd rather be one.

At age fifteen, I started an apprenticeship to become a hairdresser. You may think that's a long way from fame, fortune, glamour, and travel, yet since I have reached the age of forty-three, my friends tease me that I have created my own version of "Lifestyles of the Rich and Famous." I travel seventy percent of my life, frequently to fabulous places like Bermuda, Hawaii, the Bahamas, Orlando, and Las Vegas, addressing major corporations like AT&T and groups as large as 3,000 people. During 1984-85, I was president of the over-3,000-member National Speakers Association, the first woman to ever hold that position. In my world, that's pretty big stuff.

I'm not telling you this to impress you with my importance or achievements — it's to impress you with the *possibilities* that you can create in *your* life and all around you. Remember Woody Allen's comment that "eighty percent of life is just turning up." To me that means going out and participating in the world. You don't get discovered if you stay home. You don't fall in love without sometimes smiling at a stranger. You don't write a masterpiece until you sit down and pick up your pen. You don't become a great speaker until you have practiced before dozens and dozens of Rotary Clubs. You don't run a marathon until you call one of your pals and say, "Hey, let's go out for a brisk walk." Possibilities.

"That's Impossible"

Did you know that Debbie Fields' friends told her it was a dumb idea to open a cookie store? She said, "Maybe it is, but I won't be satisfied unless I try." She was a nervous wreck when she started her business, Mrs. Fields' Cookies.

Did you know that an ABC executive once said to Barbara Walters, "You'll never make it in broadcasting. Your energy level is wrong and you've got a speech impediment"?

Did you know that a director told Burt Reynolds, "You can't act," and told Clint Eastwood, "Your Adam's apple is too big"? As they were walking down the street afterward, Reynolds commented to Eastwood, "Well, I can learn to act, but what are you going to do?"

A young man working in a snack bar in an English theater was telling the English actors, "Hey, I'm an actor too. I'm going to make it one day." They mostly said, "Oh, sure, kid . . . and give us our sandwiches." However, when Christopher Reeve signed the contract for *Superman*, I'm sure he got a big chuckle knowing that his friends from that theater were going to find out.

"Everything I Do Is Exciting"

Sharing a limousine with Dr. Norman Vincent Peale (yes, me, with Norman Vincent Peale, after we had addressed 3,000 people — he was eighty-six years old and had more vitality and energy than you and I have put together), I asked him what was the most exciting thing in his life. He thought for a moment and mentioned traveling, his farm, and then he said, "Well, actually, Patricia, everything I do I find exciting." This proves there is possibility for joy and excitement in your life well into your eighties, but obviously you have to be *doing* something before you can become excited about doing it.

My Most Unforgettable Character

Reader's Digest features profiles of unique individuals under the heading "The Most Unforgettable Character I've Ever Met." One of my most unforgettable persons is Tricia Defibaugh. Hers is truly a rags-to-riches story.

Today Tricia is chairman of the board of Aloette Cosmetics, a big transition for a woman who got married in traditional times, determined to be a good wife, have a couple of kids, and live happily ever after. As with many couples, her husband decided that *her* dream was not *his* dream. In 1970, Tricia found herself with a three-year-old daughter and a broken marriage.

The emotional shock of the divorce was devastating. She soon realized that she had to find work, even though she had never had any desire to be a businesswoman and doubted her ability to support herself adequately. Because of her conservative Mennonite background, she was not used to the idea of women working, and she felt guilty about leaving her young daughter.

Financial need forced her to take in a boarder. She spent three years as a receptionist in a beauty salon, earning $70 a week for three days of work. Then, in exploring other part-time employment opportunities, she learned about the home-show cosmetics business. Since most of the sales demonstrations were scheduled for evenings, she could be at home with her daughter during the day and make full-time earnings by working part-time hours several evenings a week. Within one year, she was promoted to vice president of that company, and her career in beauty and sales was firmly established.

She met her present husband, John, who not only believed in her, but encouraged her to enter direct sales. Tricia and John eventually started Aloette Cosmetics.

Today Aloette is a leading force in the cosmetics home-show business both in the U.S. and abroad. In its tenth year of business, Aloette had 69 franchises in the United States, 27 in Canada, 6 in Australia, and 3 in the United Kingdom. The company has begun operating successfully in New Zealand, Hong Kong, Latin America, and the Bahamas. Tricia is the force behind Aloette's sales and marketing department. She is personally involved at least sixteen hours a day in keeping the company growing.

Aloette, based in Malvern, Pennsylvania, went public in 1986 and was cited by *INC. Magazine* as one of America's fastest-growing privately held corporations for the two consecutive years prior to the public offering. In 1987, Aloette franchises had retail sales of close to $50 million.

Tricia's and John's success did not just happen like magic. It has taken more than ten years of persistence and determination, discipline, and enthusiasm to make Aloette the company it now is, but it all began because Tricia made herself aware of the *possibilities* available to her. Tricia has discovered something she is very good at, made a science of it, and taught others how to do the same things that she does.

Tricia's story — her traditional upbringing and conservative background, her personal growth in devastating circumstances, the person she has become today — is a classic story of triumphing over adversity. It is also a story of *possibilities*.

My Second Most Unforgettable Character

Actually there are *two* people I will never forget. The second one is a man who had lost a million dollars by the time he was twenty-five years old. The story is not how he lost it, but how he made it back.

A few years ago I was hired by a gentleman in the hairstyling business. Now, I had been in the same business for twenty-four years and had made a pretty good living at it, but I could not believe what this guy had done. He and his wife had eighteen salons and had done more than $15 million in sales the year before. I was fascinated and had to learn his story.

John McCormack was not a hairdresser himself. His wife was. Years ago in New York he had been a policeman. He did a couple of entrepreneurial things like buying some Christmas trees and reselling them. But he realized that although he loved being a policeman, he had to do something else if he wanted any real economic stability.

John became a stockbroker. Times were good and he invested in some small companies that were doing well. At age twenty-five he was worth a million dollars on paper. Then the economy changed, and all the little companies he held stock in went out of business. His company folded and he was unemployed. John felt burned out, useless, lethargic. His girlfriend, Maryanne, dumped him; then she took him back. Each morning he would drive her to work, and then he would go to stare at the ocean.

So at twenty-seven John was walking down the beach, flat broke and really down. One day he met an old man on the beach who said, "Hey, young fellow, why are you so depressed?"

He replied, "I just lost a million dollars."

The old man said, "How old are you?"

"Twenty-seven."

"Well, congratulations. It took me till I was forty to lose my first million!" the old man said.

John returned to the beach every day over the next three weeks, and each time he stopped to talk with the man he calls Abe. Abe told John that he had lost everything he owned on three different occasions and learned something new each time.

John began to regain his confidence. "He had me look at all my assets and liabilities: I could speak English; I had a lot of friends; I liked numbers; I could find my way around. It was not the greatest balance sheet, but it was more than a lot of people have." Abe urged John to go to work for somebody who had started with even less than that.

John got a job with a firm that sold industrial washing machines. His boss, Bernie Milch, was Polish, a survivor of a World War II concentration camp. When he first met Milch, John was skeptical about selling washing machines and started to leave. Milch called after him, "I made $13 million last year selling washing machines." That got John's attention. John learned everything about production and sales from Milch, and, in return, he provided some financial expertise that Milch's company didn't have.

While John was out selling washing machines, he met an Italian immigrant named Nick Leone. Eventually they went into business together. Leone had been a chef before he came to America on a freighter. When the freighter docked in Philadelphia, he jumped ship. Speaking no English, he first got a job as a janitor and then as a chef. He worked hard until he was able to open his own catering business on Long Island.

Leone charged eight dollars a person for banquets and he was doing okay. Then he hired an architect to draw up plans for a beautiful banquet facility, the kind of place where people could hold large parties and gladly pay twenty dollars or more per person. Using the sketches and his vision of a greatly expanded business, Leone persuaded some of his suppliers to advance him credit. With his cash freed up, Leone built the hall. It was so successful that he soon was able to build a second one. Leone's "Italian math" inspired John: "He wasn't just a chef and he wasn't just a manager. He was a *creator*." (John and Leone are still in business together and have a lot of different projects.)

John and Maryanne got married. She was then running a successful hair salon in Valley Stream, New York. She convinced John that precision haircutting was the coming trend in the haircutting industry. They decided to establish an innovative chain of upscale, high-volume hair salons.

A common theory is that businesses fail because they do not have enough resources, but John believes that many failures occur because businesses don't set their sights high enough. In early 1976, John and Maryanne opened Visible Changes in Houston, Texas. Because of his travels as a business consultant, John had decided that Texas was the place to start. The salons would be fashionable, located in strategic shopping malls, and appeal to both men and women. The staff would be well trained in a precision haircutting technique developed by Maryanne and would be dedicated to customer service.

John worked for three years to develop an extensive and professional business plan. Even though he and Maryanne had sufficient capital to start the business, they had to make presentations to over three hundred banks before getting additional financing.

Even today, most hairstyling salons are mom-and-pop operations. All too often these small shops have poorly paid and exploited stylists who offer erratic service. Hairstyling has been a high-turnover, dead-end job with little loyalty between employer and employee. According to Bruce G. Posner and Bob Burlingham in their *INC. Magazine* profile of John McCormack, eighty percent of the haircuts done in America today are still done by businesses with only one salon. But that is changing, and John's vision is one of the reasons. He believes that the future of hairstyling lies with highly trained, highly motivated professionals who can advance within their company.

John and Maryanne interviewed nearly three hundred haircutters for their first salon. Finally they found five haircutters and a manager willing to risk the new approach. The first employees worked twelve hours a day for fifteen dollars because they believed in John's and Maryanne's dream. They knew they would share whatever success followed.

The first Houston salon offered free haircuts during its first six weeks of operations. Visible Changes, John explained, was introducing a revolutionary new haircutting system and did not want their customers to pay for it until it was perfected. The salon was a huge success.

When John and Maryanne started Visible Changes, the corporate headquarters was in their home. In 1979 they moved to more traditional offices, and in 1981, they became one of the first companies in the industry to be fully computerized. John can tell you the previous day's income at each location and compare it to other days, weeks, or months. He can show exactly how much business each employee has done, the age and sex of the customer "mix" at each location, which customers are coming back, and individual customer's birthday, anniversary, children's ages, date of last visit, and number of visits this year.

Working with his employees, John has evolved a system of commissions and bonuses that lets motivated employees earn several times more in income and benefits than they could make anywhere else. The average employee earns $33,000 a year, triple the industry average, and some make more than twice that much. Customers also get better service than they could get almost anywhere else. Each new hairstylist must achieve a twenty-five percent customer request rate within three months and a fifty percent rate within six months. If they don't, they're not Visible Changes caliber and they're out.

Company sales grew from $1.3 million in 1979 to $9.1 million in 1983. Innovative marketing techniques kept Visible Changes growing during the 1984 recession in Houston. To create a broader economic base, John set up a company to package and sell his unique computer program to other salons. He also became a partner in a business to produce and market a line of hair products sold only through salons. The hair products did $2 million of business in their first eight months. The computer programs sold $1 million worth in ten months. And in 1987, Visible Changes made $1.5 million profit on $15 million in sales. John McCormack is obviously a man alert to possibilities.

The Five Essentials of Life

There are many possibilities in your life. To take advantage of them, you need five things.

1. *Something to do*: a job, a passion, something to study, a cause to work for, a garden to dig in, a marathon to train for.

2. *Someone to love*: your mate, parents, siblings, children, friends, pets.

3. *People to share with*: all of the above, plus business associates, people who share your interests and enthusiasms, acquaintances in every walk of life.

4. *People to challenge you*: role models, mentors, people to learn from, students and apprentices (from whom you also learn), and, especially, people who disagree with you and therefore help you grow.

5. *Something to look forward to*: personal growth, positive changes, a seminar to attend, a book to read, a vacation, a movie to see, a picnic to go to. Helen Keller said, "Life is either a daring adventure or nothing at all."

Inspiring Others with Your Possibilities

Chances are that you either own or have made a gift of one of Clare Revelli's fashion products or books. But Clare almost lost her big break — until "luck" and convincing others of her possibilities gave her the boost she needed.

Before Clare started her own business, she worked as Director of Special Events at the Emporium-Capwell department store where she did the first career program for women in the country in 1979. It did very well. Macy's recruited her for a similar position. After a year with them, she decided to start her own business.

Clare took a sabbatical and wrote her first book based on the Seasonal Color Concept, a course she had been teaching at the the Fashion Institute of Design and Merchandising and at San Francisco State University. Her book, *Color and You*, came out in 1982, self-published so that she could retain full control over the color reproductions. Clare designed and wrote it as a marketing tool to explain her concept and, eventually, to sell related products. The last page of the book was a mail order form. Her firm has accumulated a mailing list from these forms, so they can notify interested readers of product lines offered in her various licensed collections.

Until 1983 Clare had a little office on Union Street and one employee who was paid when the money came in. Then *Woman's Day*, the second largest women's magazine in the country, asked her to design a color analysis kit for their readers. For $19.95, a woman could fill out the "Revelli Color Analysis Questionnaire" in the magazine, send in her $19.95, and Clare would analyze the questionnaire and mail her a Revelli color kit. Each kit contained a suede wallet, the

Revelli Personal Palette, with fabrics inside and a three-page letter from Clare explaining how to work with the woman's best colors in her wardrobe accessories and cosmetics. The kit also included a national brands makeup guide and a copy of Clare's book, *Color and You*. Because of their huge readership, *Woman's Day* asked Clare to prepare approximately ten thousand kits in advance. That involved an enormous amount of money up front.

"I was a single woman renting a small apartment here in San Francisco and had only a fifteen-year-old car for collateral on a bank loan. Not much, right? I needed $25,000 start-up money, but every bank I approached turned me down.

"Then, as fashion editor for the *Nob Hill Gazette*—I always had freelance jobs on the side—I was covering the opening of the new Louis Vuitton store in San Francisco when I struck up a conversation with a nice woman. She turned out to be a loan officer at a local bank! We found we had a lot in common—she also was a native San Franciscan of Italian origin—and we decided to have lunch together the following week.

"On Monday I called her at the bank to arrange lunch. At first she couldn't place me, then suddenly she said, 'Oh, yes, you're the fashion editor who needs a bank loan.' By the time I took her to lunch, she had looked over all my books and noticed that I had no collateral. She said, 'There's only one way you're going to get a loan. Do exactly what I tell you. I'm going to inform my bosses upstairs that I'm putting your loan through—*after* I have given you the money. Now, fill out these forms. Your loan is going to be rejected, but I really believe in you and your program. I am willing to take this chance.'

"The next morning, on her instructions, I went to her bank and withdrew the $25,000 I needed to set up the *Woman's Day* kits. The day after that, her bosses did in fact stamp 'rejected' on my loan application, telling her it was was 'fraught with peril'!

"The *Woman's Day* promotion was successful beyond my wildest dreams. When it broke on the newsstands, we got approximately 8,000 orders in the first ten days. By the time the program finished a year and a half later—and mind you this was a one-time February 1984 issue—they had received over 30,000 orders at $20 per order. Everyone involved made a great deal of money."

Clare could still be organizing department store fashion shows and Easter egg hunts (and that's not a bad thing to be doing), but because she believed in her own possibilities and got others to believe in them, she achieved much, much more in the fashion and beauty industries. Clare's *Color and You* (Simon & Schuster) has sold 3 million copies to date. In addition, she has written promotional books on haircoloring: *Colors of Your Life* for Clairol, which has sold 50,000 copies; *Color Sense* for No Nonsense with 4 million copies; and more recently *Focus on Color* for Ralston Purina, 2 million copies sold so far.

Clare also has an assortment of licensees: silk scarfs, eyeglasses, belts, jewelry, and even a software computer program. All products are nationally distributed and labeled with the Revelli name.

And if all this were not enough, she has licensed her name to a forthcoming video based on her book called "Color and You," marketed by Simon & Schuster and distributed by Paramount. Clare's latest venture is *Making News*, a nationally distributed full-color newsletter on fashion, color, and beauty.

Some people would call Clare lucky, but it's the kind of luck we've been talking about—the luck that doesn't happen unless you are out there plugging away, exploring your possibilities. Clare recognized her possibilities and convinced others to back her. Her contract with *Woman's Day* magazine and her chance meeting with the bank loan officer were *opportunities* for her to succeed.

Possibilities in a New Land

Nicole Schapiro was just a baby when her parents were imprisoned in a concentration camp during World War II. Friends hid the child during the war. Both her parents miraculously survived and went in search of Nicole. They found her, but the beautiful, bouncy baby girl they had left eight years before was now a mute, withdrawn nine-year-old.

Desperate for anything that would help restore the bright, energetic child she remembered, Nicole's mother sent her to mime school. About the same time, Nicole found an old book about America in the basement of her home in Hungary, a book full of marvelous stories about this distant country. The Communist regime had made it illegal to possess anything printed by American publishers, but Nicole treasured this book and read the stories over and over. She decided that she was going to be an American.

In 1957 the Hungarian Revolution broke out, and Nicole learned how to make Molotov cocktails. She was caught along with twenty-one other young people and lined up with them to be shot. Nicole was fifteen and all the executioners were no older. Of the group, only Nicole survived. When she looks back she asks herself, "How come?" She remembers that for a single instant, she and the Russian soldier with rifle raised to kill her looked at each other. They seemed to think together that "This is crazy, why are we doing this?"

She escaped death, and was more determined than ever to leave for America, but the American consulate said the quota was frozen — America didn't want any more Hungarians. So she spent one month standing in front of the consulate until she became an eyesore. She became an experienced bag lady, and finally she got attention. They said, "She really wants to go."

Eventually she appealed to President Eisenhower. She wrote, "We both have the same vision. We both love America and want it to be a free and equal country. Freedom is not that we are able to get everything we want. Freedom is that you can become whatever you want to become. What I can do, if you let me in, is I will be able to influence people. I want to influence people all over the world to feel like you do."

What Nicole sought was the chance, the *possibility* of doing the best she could do, of making a difference for herself and others. During her career in America she has been a vice president of sales and marketing for Citibank in New York, and today is a top speaker and seminar leader influencing people around the country — just as she promised Eisenhower she would. She keeps an onion on her desk because once when she was a little girl, her mother had been too poor to make her a birthday cake. Instead they took an onion and pretended it was a cake. Now the onion reminds her of where she's been and of the opportunities that open up when you are alert to possibilities.

YOUR ASSIGNMENT:
What Are My Possibilities?

Three things that I'd really like to do, but which are absolutely, utterly *impossible* are:

1. _____

2. _____

3. _____

Three things I'd really like to do that would be easy if I just tried are:

1. _____

2. _____

3. _____

What items from the impossible list do I want to reconsider?

What items from the easy list do I want to go for?

CHAPTER 17

When Things Go Wrong

> *"Alas! How easily things go wrong!"*
>
> George MacDonald

"How many of you have had things go wrong in your business that seemed devastating at the time?" I asked an audience of Women Entrepreneurs in San Francisco. Everyone raised a hand. Some people put up *two* hands.

I have had a wonderful business, great employees, and many successes. I have also been disappointed, had hard-earned funds embezzled, had people quit at the most inopportune moments, and managed to live through every single experience, and *grow from it*.

It's easy to look back at business disappointments and realize, as Larry Wilson says, that they were just inconvenient. Wilson, author of *One Minute Salesman*, believes that most business traumas will turn out to be merely inconveniences or even springboards to something better when seen in perspective. Businesses run in cycles, up and down. When you survive a few cycles, you are a lot more valuable to your clients. I serve my audience better, not because of any success I've had, but because of my *ability to adapt*.

Adversity in business can be a springboard for creative thinking and new growth. One man, for example, found himself with a warehouse full of canned white salmon. Housewives, used to the pink kind, wouldn't touch it until he had new labels printed: Snow-white Alaskan Salmon — guaranteed not to turn pink in the can. Such switch tactics can also backfire. Recently a manufacturer made up thousands of Oliver North dolls when the Colonel first came to prominence for shredding sensitive documents during the Iran/Contra scandals. When the story faded from the front pages and the dolls languished unsold, the manufacturer repackaged them without North's name. Then North was indicted and aroused new public interest.

Great thinkers and creative people throughout history have thrived in periods when their work had some sort of restriction put on it: political, financial, or cultural. The symphony and the sonnet are very rigid forms, yet we have an abundance of great symphonies and sonnets. Great works have been produced in hard times, in the midst of hunger, calamity, and oppression. Sometimes a disaster can simply be a restriction that channels us and simplifies our choices.

What if the adversity is physical? Oscar-winning actress Susan Hayward, Olympic skater Scott Hamilton, and Steven DeVore, president of SyberVision, all had polio as children. They each retrained their bodies until they were able to perform better than most people with no such handicap. DeVore has used his experience to produce a system of videotape models that people can use to improve their performance in various sports. For Hayward, Hamilton, and DeVore, adversity was their spur, not their shackle.

The One-Armed Ball Player

Boo Bue told me the story of George Quam. Boo met George at the Minneapolis Athletic Club in 1961. As a boy, George and his two brothers roamed all over their Minnesota farm. A railroad spur crossed one corner of the property, and George's mother constantly warned her children not to go near the tracks. But as most kids do, George did.

When George was about eight years old, he and his brother were on top of a boxcar playing cowboys and Indians. All of a sudden, a switch engineer hit the cars and George fell between two moving boxcars. Before he could scamper off the track, one of the cars severed his left arm. Quam told Boo, "I was handicapped. If there was any doubt in my mind, that doubt was erased every Saturday when I went to town and behind my back heard everyone say, 'There goes the poor Quam boy. Isn't it a shame the way he's handicapped?'"

"Well," Quam said, "handicapped was exactly how I felt. That was my attitude. I didn't have any goals or dreams. I had trouble communicating. I became a loner. Then one day my dad said, 'George, you're going to do the same chores around here your brothers are doing.' I started doing things and one day I realized I could do everything with one hand that my brothers could do with two. My life was never the same."

In high school George liked sports. He got letters in football, basketball, and baseball, three years in a row. After high school he moved to Minneapolis and got a room in a downtown YMCA. He went into real estate and insurance work, and was very successful.

One day he saw some people playing handball. He had never seen the game before, so he went down to the handball court and began hitting the ball. He was awkward, but he could do it. About fifteen minutes later, the athletic director of the YMCA came by, saw George, and said, "You can't play handball with one arm! It takes two hands, two arms, a lot of coordination. You ought to take up something like chess or bridge where you can use your mind." George was devastated. That night he didn't sleep, he cried. But the next morning he swore to himself that he was going to play handball.

He got the best players in the club to show him how to make the kill shots into the corners. In three years he was the Class A singles champion of the Minneapolis YMCA. Then he started playing at the Minneapolis Athletic Club where the competition was even keener...and he set an amazing record. He was the Singles Champion in Class A play for twenty-five straight years.

When Boo met George, Boo was thirty-eight years old and George was sixty-three. "We had just finished playing two games of handball," Boo recalls. "I had some advantages over him. I was younger, I had two arms and two hands, and I could play the game—I had three trophies in my den from the Minneapolis Athletic Club. Yet he beat me 21-4, 21-5, and I think he gave me all nine points. In other words, he murdered me. And I said to him, 'George, I figured you'd beat me, but I didn't think you'd beat me this easily.' He said, 'Well, I have a big advantage over you. Every time you went over to the left, you wondered whether you should hit the ball with your left hand or backhand with your right. I never have to take the time to make that decision.'

"To me, it was a remarkable way of doing what Dale Carnegie says, 'When life hands you a lemon, make lemonade.' George made a positive out of a negative. As we left the athletic club that day, I said, 'George, what's your philosophy of life?' I'll never forget his answer. He said, 'Boo, it's not what you have that counts, but what you do with what you have.'"

The Woman Who Changed the Law

Susan Helmrich and I met on an airplane flying to Toronto. It turned out that she had planned to hear me speak two nights before, but hadn't made it. We talked nonstop for five hours until the plane landed, the first time I've ever done this. Susan is one of those spunky people who got a raw deal in life. Instead of withdrawing into self-pity, she fought to help others in the same situation.

Susan was twenty-one years old, attending college on an athletic scholarship. "I felt fine, although I had had lots of gynecologic problems. The day the doctor told me I had cancer, I was sure that he had me mixed up with another patient. It couldn't be me. He said, "Yes." And I said, "Is it serious?" He said, "Yes." And I said, "Will I be able to have children?" He said, "No." That's when I cried. When you're twenty-one and you have your whole life ahead of you, you can't imagine what losing this option is like. Two weeks later I had ten hours of surgery at Sloane Kettering."

Susan learned that she was a "DES daughter," one of a group of cancer-prone women whose mothers had taken the drug diethylstilbestrol — DES — in the 1950s. DES was then commonly prescribed to prevent miscarriage during pregnancy, although it was never tested for this use and was found to be totally ineffective in preventing miscarriage. At first Susan concentrated on surviving from day to day.

"When all that is happening to you, you don't think about lawsuits or of suing anyone. All you can think about is getting well. I spent one month in the hospital, and after that I had two subsequent major abdominal surgeries. It was a long hard road, but somehow you keep on going. I was hospitalized ten times in three years. Every time I started to feel good and think I was cured, I'd end up back in the hospital with complications. But, I had lots of support. My family, my friends, and my doctors and nurses were always there for me, and helped me a lot.

"When I decided to go to graduate school, people were incredulous. But you can sit in your room by yourself for the rest of your life, or you can get on with your life."

In 1978 Susan started her master's degree at Harvard in epidemiology. She also tried to file a lawsuit against the manufacturers of DES. She learned that, under New York state law, the statute of limitations had run out. In 1979 she and other DES daughters began lobbying to change the law.

"We started as six women. We quickly realized that we weren't strong enough to fight the New York State Senate. We had to gather more support. We used media coverage, and joined the Toxic Victims Coalition, which included those exposed to asbestos and other harmful substances."

As Susan's political savvy grew, she also learned how to cope with her own feelings. "An important thing is to allow yourself to cry. Acknowledge that it's a horrible thing that you're going through. Finally, I was able to say, 'This is horrible; I hate this; I'm depressed.' I had felt that I had to be strong for everybody else, but that's not true. You have to be strong for yourself. I've grown a lot because if I could endure that, I know I can do anything."

Each year Susan's lobbying group was faced with new barriers, but year after year they slowly gathered support from other organizations. By 1985 they had the support of the AFL-CIO and many victims of toxic exposures.

"My wedding was scheduled for June 15, but I spent the early part of June 1986 lobbying in Albany. It seemed as though another year would end in defeat. Then I got married and left for my honeymoon in Hawaii with my new husband. Our second day there, we got a phone call that the bill had passed. It seemed like a fantasy because here we were off on this beautiful island. I couldn't believe it.

"A few weeks later I was asked to fly to New York for the bill-signing ceremony with Governor Cuomo and Robert Abrams, attorney general of New York. Two other victims were asked to be present: an asbestos widow and a man with heavy metal disease. The day of the bill signing was a day that I'll never forget. I saw the culmination of six years of hard work. I was talking to the media about having had cancer and having had my vagina and uterus removed, and never being able to have children, and so on. I cried when the bill was signed because I was ecstatic and I was also sad that the whole reason I was there was because I had had cancer and all these terrible things had happened to me. But the new law allows me to seek compensation.

"I've done things that I never would have done if this hadn't happened to me. My career has suffered somewhat because I've been sidetracked into doing other things, but I got my master's degree from Harvard. I had a good job and have published papers and done research. Now I'm in a doctoral program at the University of California, Berkeley, School of Public Health, studying epidemiology. Looking back, the legislative work that I did has been the most rewarding of my life because I was able to help change a law that will affect thousands and thousands of people. And that's a really good feeling."

The Ultimate Loss

Judith Briles is the successful author of five books, *The Dollars and Sense of Divorce*, *A Woman's Guide to Financial Savvy*, *Money Phases*, *Woman to Woman: From Sabotage to Support*, and *Faith and Savvy*. She is also someone who has fought her way back from two major losses. Several years ago her business partner embezzled over half a million dollars that Judith had to cover, and she lost her her home, cars, and every asset she had.

The second loss was more devastating. Her nineteen-year-old son, Frank, died in a tragic accident. He had gone to the movies with some friends. Climbing on the old Dumbarton Bridge in the San Francisco Bay afterward, he somehow misstepped and toppled over the side. He hit a girder on the way down, and then was swept away in the treacherous currents of the Bay. It was seven weeks before his body was recovered.

"Frank was the kind of kid whose gift to me on Mother's Day was cleaning his room," Judith recalls. "Our life felt pretty good. Frank had a bank account, had saved some money, and was going to buy a new motorcycle. It was Labor Day weekend. He was going to be signing his loan papers on Tuesday. We had dinner, then he and his friends all went off to the movies. At 1:00 A.M. I got up and saw that my youngest daughter's door was still open. My first thought was to wring her neck because she had no business being out that late. Frank's door was closed and so was my oldest daughter's door, so I assumed they were both in. I went back to bed.

Two hours later I bolted straight up. My younger daughter was at the foot of the bed and I remember saying, 'What do you mean, Frank is in the morgue?' She led me down the hallway, into the brightly lit family room where a lone policeman stood. He said, 'I'm sorry, there's been an accident.'

"Because I was well known, the story was all over the newspapers. I couldn't retreat into private grief the way I had when I lost a newborn baby years before. And there were ten friends with Frank when he died, including his younger sister. We had a lot of work to do with these young people to help them deal with their first tragedy.

"As time went by, I continued to withdraw. I'd go into work, but I was encased in a shell. It was strange. Everyone assumed I was doing well, but I wasn't doing well at all. It was a long time before anyone realized the crisis that had encircled me. I was in the middle of my studies for my doctorate, and I was having nightmares about Frank.

"I had reached a state in which I couldn't remember to do anything. I couldn't remember to carry a checkbook with me to pay for things. I couldn't remember to pay bills. My phone would get cut off. I would drive across the Bay and I couldn't even remember to bring change for the toll to come home again. I needed a keeper. But my outgoing personality precluded anyone from realizing how bad off I had become.

"My daughters had been ready to move out, go off on their own. We decided to all hang together. My relationship with my husband, John, Frank's stepfather, was deeply strained. I was angry at him for all the things I thought he hadn't done with Frank. Later I realized that John had done his best, but we had to spend a long time rebuilding our relationship. Now we're probably the best we've ever been. What came out of that tragedy could have wiped everything out, but it didn't.

"During that journey, my son left me three gifts: first, a renewed spirituality; second, his joyous sense of being a little kid. I've taken that as part of myself now. I mean I really want to have fun. I like having fun. I've always liked having fun, but now I'm serious about having fun. And third, touching base with and reaffirming my own values.

"I've had a lot of growth since that time, and I have learned from my own personal situation that no matter how much money I might lose, how badly my career may be hurt, it doesn't matter. Family counts most. Nothing else could hurt me. I have my priorities in the correct order now. I closed out my last doctoral class with this motto: 'Don't do well what you have no business doing.' And I have remembered that. It is imprinted on my brain."

Judith Briles is now working on two new books, one called *In Search of Self-Confidence*, the other, *When God Says No*, on the death of her son and on her journey through pain to joy. Her ordeal demonstrates three points about surviving great loss:

1. Any great loss involves loss of part of yourself, so realize it will take time to rebuild.

2. You *can* rebuild.

3. Loss can force you to redefine your priorities and goals, to refocus and renew.

The Road Back

Author/lecturer Joan Minninger was devastated when her husband and business partner died. Although she carried on so that few noticed any change, she was really operating on "automatic." After two years, she recognized that she was ready to start again. She threw a party and invited all the people who had ever hired her, ostensibly to thank them but privately to celebrate that her grieving was over. The party was a tremendous success on both fronts.

YOUR ASSIGNMENT:
What would I do if my world falls apart?

If tragedy struck tomorrow, how would I cope?

What resources — friends, family, beliefs, inner strengths — would I find the most helpful?

CHAPTER 18

Health

"A good mechanic may be needed for body repair, but you, the owner of your body, must know how to do the trouble-shooting."

William M. Buchholz, M.D.

What is the exercise/nutrition/antistress mania all about? The answer is simple: It's all about better physical health and better mental health as well. It's very difficult to be a dynamic success if you don't feel well.

American Health magazine reports that more and more Americans are discovering that "taking charge of your health relates to your general sense of well-being *more strongly than any other variable*, including your salary. . . . Increasingly we're realizing that a positive mental attitude and a feeling of having control over your life are essential to mental and physical well-being."

Stress on the Job

In the final days of the American Civil War, Ulysses S. Grant was pursuing Robert E. Lee across Virginia. Grant ordered Lee to surrender, but Lee refused. The opposing armies took up camps near Appomattox Court House.

Grant wrote in his diary that he was suffering from a sick headache, that he had sat up all night bathing his feet, wrists, and neck with hot mustard and water. At dawn the next day, Grant was still in misery. Then a messenger arrived with a note from General Lee. Lee was willing to surrender. "When the officer reached me," Grant wrote,

"I was still suffering from the sick headache, but the instant I saw the contents of the note I was cured."

Your Job Can Make You Sick

"Do you think a bad boss can make you sick?" Ken Blanchard asked an audience in San Francisco. We muttered something about "probably." Ken said, "Absolutely yes." But being sick doesn't come from the difficulty of the situation, it comes from failing to deal with the stress—from the debilitating tension of unresolved and unconfronted conflict.

The former employer of my friend Rosie had that effect on her. Rosie was often expected to run business errands on her own time on the way to work, but still had to be in her seat at nine o'clock on the dot. She would be given instructions, only to have them contradicted later in front of a client so it appeared that she had ignored company policy. She was expected to stretch the truth to clients when it suited her employer's purposes, but if she was caught, she was never backed up by her employer and was made to look like the guilty party.

Not surprisingly Rosie began suffering severe neck pain and muscle spasms. At one point she could not raise her right arm. One day after bending over to pick up a pencil, she could not straighten up. She was treated by a chiropractor, a masseuse, and an acupressurist—without much success. When alcohol and drugs loomed as the next solution, she decided to take a much more healthful and logical step: end the tension that was making her sick by finding a less frustrating, more rewarding job. Since that day, she has not suffered one physical symptom from stress.

Need More Sleep? Get Married

When I was a hairstylist, one of my regular clients who was a very carefree bachelor told me he was getting married. "Why?" I asked. "You're giving up the fun life you've been telling me about for years!"

In all seriousness he said, "Patricia, I am competing in business with people who get eight hours of sleep a night!"

If you are serious about your career, these things make a difference. You are competing in business and life with people who are dynamic and healthy, whose lifestyle gives them energy. Maybe it's time you gave them a run for their money!

Confessions of an Indoor Girl

My family was totally nonathletic. I left school at fifteen, vowing never to do anything athletic again. No more hockey. No more netball. I hated them all. Besides, I didn't like being cold. My fingernails were too long, and the other girls were all so much bigger than I. I honestly believed that you didn't have to worry too much about your body. With good "all-in-one" foundation garments, anyone could look great in clothes.

But in 1969 I gave up smoking, joined a gym, started exercising and studying nutrition, and cleared up my eating act a bit. I didn't get really serious about being athletic, however, until I was around thirty-five. My hairstyling business was doing well, and my speaking career was progressing. It wasn't that I didn't feel proud of myself, but all my activities were directed toward work and career. I felt that I had to do something to prove to myself — not the world — that I could do or be *anything* I wanted. I made a list of the most unbelievable, unnatural things I could think of.

The first item, being a brain surgeon, was rather intriguing but unrealistic. Fortunately brain surgery didn't appeal to me much. The next most unnatural thing on my list was to be athletic. I decided I was going to be a runner. That certainly was a challenging goal. Apart from doing a few exercises, I had never attempted anything like it before.

Running fit all the criteria for good goals. It seemed *attainable* — I was in fairly good shape, had arms and legs, and was not much overweight. It was a *measurable* goal, all right, because I could calculate my progress. I took the next step: I *co-authored* my goal. I asked all my pals who ran whether I could join them. If anyone asked me to lunch with them, I'd say, "No, but do you run?" My good friend Eileen O'Connell became my trainer for my informal first half-marathon. Seven friends supported me, running from the Ferry Building in San Francisco over the Golden Gate Bridge to Fred's Place in Sausalito, an absolutely spectacular run of about thirteen miles.

Once a week I would call another friend, Bert Decker, and tell him how many miles I had run the week before. If I was out of town, my staff would call him. (The fact is, he probably didn't care at all, but checking in with someone kept me feeling committed.)

Making Your Own Health Plan

How do you start? You might begin by reading books on nutrition and exercise. Here are some good ones:

Get Well Naturally by Linda Clark, ARC Giant Book.

Let's Get Well by Adele Davis, Signet.

Look Younger, Live Longer by Gaylord Hauser, Fawcett-Crest.

Nutrition and Your Mind by George Watson, Harper & Row.

Total Fitness in 30 Minutes by Laurence E. Morehouse and Leonard Gross, Simon & Schuster.

Women and Fatigue by Holly Atkinson, G. P. Putnam's Sons.

A recent Gallup poll reported that as many as 69 percent of Americans now exercise. According to the poll, "[The] numbers should put to rest, once and for all, any notion that fitness is a fad or a trend that's already peaked."

Remember that any exercise you choose has to be fun and something that you enjoy, so you will keep it up. Take a small amount of exercise regularly. Don't let yourself sit around all week and then try to make up for it by exercising vigorously for six hours on the weekend. You'll be sore, sorry, and may injure yourself seriously.

Exercise is always better with company, especially at the start. Get a friend to join you. Going to a gym is a great way to meet new people with common interests, to expand your circle of friends. (Although running is popular right now, it's not for everyone. Don't feel bad if you don't like it. There are dozens of other ways to stretch and tone your body.)

Get up early. Since the early morning belongs to so few people in the world, take advantage of that time of day when you probably have the most energy. It's a wonderful way to set up the day.

Whenever you feel like a beer or a doughnut, try going for a walk, run, jog, or swim. Arrange to meet people for exercise instead of calorie-filled coffee breaks, lunches, or dinners. Pack your own light lunch — an apple and a whole wheat sandwich or yogurt — and spend the rest of the time exercising, rather than going to a restaurant.

Guard your rest periods as rigorously as you guard your work periods. The only time I get negative or down is when I'm overtired. Then I have a tendency to overeat as well. To be more productive, take time to recharge your batteries and renew yourself. When you look at your desk and don't know where to begin, go to the movies, soak in a bubblebath, or go to bed early, and tackle it first thing in the morning.

For mental health, have a list of the things you really enjoy doing. Usually they're very simple. I love to read, knit, make a batch of muffins, call my mother or my friends. I don't know that it's realistic to think that we can "have it all." Instead take time for yourself and realize how much you already have.

Take the time to realize why you are keeping yourself mentally and physically healthy. When you have priorities, it's much easier to stay on track.

Fighting Fatigue

All the talk about becoming physically fit and totally healthy means little if you are too tired to fight anything anymore, let alone fatigue. Many women are simply too tired, says Holly Atkinson in *Women and Fatigue*. "Women today [are] . . . substantially overworked," says Dr. Atkinson. Her book is full of tips for combating fatigue. I recommend it to anyone who drags around feeling tired much of the time.

Starting a Home Exercise Program

If you've been relatively sedentary, don't rush out and buy lots of expensive exercise equipment. It will end up sitting in a closet, a source of clutter and guilt. Instead, ease into your new regimen slowly.

Begin by getting your spouse or a friend to go for a walk with you. Make this a pleasurable routine. When you both notice how much better you feel, how your brains are clearer (this has been demonstrated in scientific tests), how you are able to relax better and sleep better, then you can probably persuade your partner to add some simple calisthenics, maybe to an exercise video. Keep stretching your body and your routine until you have a full-fledged exercise program. Consult the experts as you go. I especially recommend *Total Fitness in 30 Minutes* by Laurence E. Morehouse and Leonard Gross.

Exercise offers other benefits beside physical fitness. It is a wonderful time for camaraderie with spouse or friends. My early morning runs with my different running partners are quality times in my life. Out of all that sweat have come the closest relationships I have.

Walking with your mate can even offer some benefits you may not have imagined. In *How to Make Love to the Same Person for the Rest of Your Life and Enjoy It,* Dagmar O'Connor describes the remarkable cure of a loving couple who had stopped having sex. These two people were both a little overweight and they smoked. They were generally run-down and "too tired." O'Connor told them to go for a walk together every evening. The first day, after a brisk twenty-minute walk, they came home and the wife got in the shower first. The husband got in before she got out, and they were soaping each other and you can guess what happened next. This became the highlight of the day for them—they couldn't wait to get home to shower together. Their problem was solved.

The Lady and the Body Builders

The only thing Sharon Hanes Brown ever exercised in her life was good taste. In 1987 she decided to take up body building. "Why, I don't know!" she said. "People seem to do strange things after they turn forty." Sharon went at it seriously and contacted a trainer. He took her to a serious gym, the kind where you are looked at with suspicion if you ever wash your gym clothes.

"My trainer was a big guy. He'd take me up to a piece of equipment, show me what to do with it, and I'd do it. Then we'd go to the next piece. All I had to do was go in there and do what he said.

"I'll tell you a couple of principles of body building. It's all about 'sets' and 'reps.' Let's say I'm going to do squats. I get this bar and put it on the back of my shoulder. I stand there and I do six of those. That's one set of six reps.

"Soon I graduated—I was ready to be on my own. I packed my little gym bag and off to the gym I went. I walked in and looked around and thought, Oh, my goodness.

"First of all, I didn't realize that all the equipment would be in use by these big, big guys. They hadn't looked so big before because my trainer would just walk over and take charge of a machine. What was I going to do now? I mean these guys are something. They've got these huge, huge muscles on their arms, and their legs are so big they can't put them together. They give each other these little remarks of encouragement and brotherhood: Right on, brother, right on. I mean they are *cool.* They walk into that gym and people scatter. They're the kings there, and everybody gets out of their way. What am I going to do? I thought. I would just wait around and after about fifteen minutes I'd find a piece of equipment that was free and I'd scurry over.

"I was on the squat rack again and out of the corner of my eye I see this big guy standing over there staring. Now, can you imagine how self-conscious that made me feel? When I went to get my next weight from the rack, he walks over and says, 'How many more sets you got?' I said, 'Oh, I'm finished, thank you.'

"I threw my clothes in the bag and left there, cursing myself all the way home. I thought, This is crazy. I'm forty- two years old and I let somebody like that intimidate me? But I was committed. The next day I went right back in there.

"And that's when my whole world changed. I was sitting on the life cycle reading my Iaccoca, and it hit me! I suddenly realized what these body builders' purpose was in life, why they existed. I thought, Oh, my gosh, their purpose in life, their *sole* purpose, was to inspire people like me!

"I noticed that they didn't go to any secret room back there with a star on it and do secret things. I did bicep curls, they did bicep curls. I did squats, they did squats. That's when I realized that if I came to that gym every day and did what they did, I could look just like them. What role models. Then I wasn't afraid of anything.

"Some of the body builders—the ones who were really obnoxious and rude—hadn't realized they were there to inspire me. Did I care? No, it didn't matter. *I* knew.

"There was another kind of body builder there too, the kind who would come over and say, 'Excuse me, the way you're holding your hands on that bar leaves you open for injury. You need to move your hands just a little bit. Then you'll be able to grow and you won't be injured.' Now, is that not the sweetest thing? These body builders knew the third 'C' to success, *concern* for other people. They knew that once you reach a certain level, there's always somebody just a little lower who doesn't know what you know.

"You have a responsibility to turn around and give away your success. All of the greats know this. Where would we be today if it weren't for Leonardo da Vinci, Plato, Einstein, and all of those others who never knew a squat from a press, but who passed down their information to us freely, beautifully, so that we could progress too ?

"There's nothing that you might want to do that you can't go to a library or a school to find out, or talk to someone who is willing to give you that information. That's what concern is all about. Concern is 'synergy' which the dictionary defines as 'an action of two or more organisms to produce an effect of which each individually is incapable.' One plus one equals three. It's all win. No 'zero-sum' nonsense here. You can reach your goals at the same time I'm reaching mine."

Thank you, Sharon Hanes Brown!

Indulge in a Health Spa

If you can, take a week off and go to a health spa. Even if you can only manage a weekend, that's a good start.

My favorite is The Palms at Palm Springs. It's owned by a woman named Sheila Cluff, who also owns The Oaks at Ojai, which offers a similar program but in a different setting.

What happens at a health spa? Usually you can do as much or as little as you wish. A typical day starts at 7:00 A.M. with a three-mile brisk walk or, for slow starters, a more leisurely one-mile walk. Classes in stretching, aerobics, weight loss, and nutrition follow. The spa helps you to take a good look at how you choose to live your life and set your goals.

I usually go with my cronies. Even alone, I always feel at home at a spa. The food is always fantastic, 750 to 1,100 calories a day. I go to a spa at least twice a year to get back on track and to remind me of how I choose to live my life.

Turning Around for a Healthy Mind

A friend I made through running was David Leof, who is a psychiatrist. One day we jogged from the Marina Green to the Golden Gate Bridge and back again. We were walking to cool down, out past the Saint Francis Yacht Club. The sky was clear and full of seagulls, the water was blue and full of boats. As we turned back toward our car, we saw the greenery and the trees, and the bridge, and the joggers stretching.

David said, "You see what we've just done, Patricia? We have just turned around a few degrees, and it looks as if we're looking at two totally different cities. The good thing about my practice is that people only have to change their thinking a few degrees to have totally different lives."

We've all heard people say, "Well, it's not working where I am. I think I'm going to move to another state, divorce my spouse, sell my children, go into a different line of business, lose fifty pounds, or bleach my hair blonde, and then my life will work." When it comes to good mental health, sometimes we just have to realize what we have to be grateful for, and just change our thinking a few degrees. When you have a good relationship with your body, it's easier to keep a good state of mind.

YOUR ASSIGNMENT:
My Relationship With My Body

Stress

[ ] I usually deal with stress very well.

[ ] I need to learn to deal with stress
better. To do this, I will _____

_____

Diet

[ ] My diet is nourishing and contains all the essential vitamins and
minerals. I eat appropriate amounts from each food group,
balance my fats, proteins and carbohydrates, and get the right
number of calories.

[ ] I need to learn more about food. I will_____

_____

[ ] I know all that stuff but I'm too lazy or distracted to eat properly.
From now on, I will _____

_____

Exercise

[ ] I exercise regularly and am in great shape.

[ ] I need to exercise more. From now on, I will_____

_____

CHAPTER 19

Your Love Affair With Life

"If a man has a talent and cannot use it, he has failed. If he has a talent and uses only half of it, he has partly failed. If he has a talent and learns somehow to use the whole of it, he has gloriously succeeded, and won a satisfaction and a triumph few men ever know."

Thomas Wolfe,
The Web and the Rock

More than anything else, people ask me, "How can I know what I want? I'm intelligent and well educated," they say. "I have a good job and am not unattractive. But how can I know what I want?"

My reply is a question. "If in five years you are doing exactly what you're doing now, in the same job, with the same company, with the same friends — if you look the same, and you spend your free time doing the same things — would you be happy?" If the answer is no, then the question becomes "What would make you happy?"

If you don't want to look the way you do now, what goals can you set about losing or gaining weight, developing better muscle tone, better grooming, a new outlook reflected in the clothes you wear and how you wear them? If you don't like certain character traits (like impatience — I must work on this characteristic daily), what can you do to change them? You don't have to set monumental goals to make a difference in your life.

If you would not be happy in the same job five years from now, look within your company or organization for other jobs. Are there

other departments? Higher positions? Could you create a new department or position? How far can you go? If you like the possibilities in
your company, figure out what you have to learn, whom you have to
impress, whom you have to know, and what you have to do. If you are
not satisfied with the possibilities in your organization, look around
your field. Is there anything there for you? Think about your talents,
your abilities, your interests. What other things could you do? Talk to
people in other industries.

Take Inventory

If you don't have a strong sense of your talents and interests,
have your abilities tested to determine your aptitudes. Are you
mechanically minded? Are you analytically inclined? Do you work well
with numbers? Are you creative? Do you like to work with other
people? Do you like to work alone? These are the things you must know
about yourself.

Think about your personal life. Are you happy single or married?
How would you like your personal and social life to be different? How
can you make your marriage, your family, your living situation better?

The important thing is to *think*. And as Leo Rosten once said in
the *Saturday Review*, "Thinking is harder work than hard work."

On her fortieth birthday, one of my friends, Linda Levine, vice
president of Kidder Peabody, went away to a beautiful seaside town
and spent four days just thinking about what she wanted to do during
the next ten years of her life. Most people never take time to think
about the future. They take the time to go skiing, to go sailing, to watch
television, but they do not take time to think about what they want.
This is something we should all do on a fairly regular basis, not just
every decade or so.

Have a Love Affair

People in love secrete extra hormones that make the whole world
seem rosier. Having a love affair with your job offers the same benefits
(and some of the drawbacks) as the person-to-person love affair. It goes
through the same three stages.

Remember how exciting it was when you first fell in love? Your
heart did somersaults every time you met the object of your affection.
The two of you sat up talking all night, and you always seemed to have
so much energy. The thrill of falling in love was wonderful.

Soon enough, reality set in and you had to start working to make the relationship succeed. That's good, of course. It's how you grow to truly know and love the other person.

In many ways, a new job is also a love affair. The first stage, excitement, can last from one hour to many years. You think to yourself: This job will pay me more money than I've ever earned before; the clients will be wonderful to deal with; and I'm going to learn so much and do exciting things. The novelty of the job keeps your energy high, and you are very productive because you are happy. In fact, being productive makes you happy.

Then the second stage, reality, begins to set in. You still enjoy the work, but you find that you don't like getting up early every morning. You come into an office of madly ringing phones. You feel that you barely have time to get everything accomplished. In short, the novelty wears off.

Like love, your job has a third stage too: looking. You're too centered in reality. All you notice are the bad things about your situation. That's when the maybe's begin. "*Maybe* I could make better money at Company X and not have to work so hard," you say. "*Maybe* I'd be happier with more responsibility in Corporation Y. *Maybe* Company Z would let me come in a little later in the morning."

If you're like most people, you approach your job realistically. You know that everything can't always be right, but you feel pretty good about most of the things you do. But one day you begin to criticize everything. Just as you put the blame in a relationship on someone else, in a job you come to believe it somehow has failed you. Do you think your job has failed?

Ask yourself a few simple questions. Are you giving 100 percent? Are you causing your own problems, perhaps to find a little excitement? Are you optimistic about your job? Are you worried about the future of your company and the part you play in it? Do you feel unappreciated?

Why did you take that job in the first place? What were the things that first attracted you? Are they still a part of your daily experience? Why don't they thrill you anymore? Are they really different, or is it only your attitude toward them that has changed?

Pretend You Own the Company

The most important thing your job can offer you is a good feeling about yourself. Do you see yourself as a productive, contributing member of the company? Do you know why your company exists? When you realize what your company offers to society, you'll be able to understand better what part you play.

Robert Townsend advised people to work with the attitude that they owned the company that employed them. You earn your money from your employer by doing *more* than you are paid to do. According to the "law of sow and reap," you will get noticed for being an exceptional worker, so don't worry about giving your employers "something for nothing." More important, you'll feel good about yourself because you will be a productive person with a part in your company's future. Reaping the rewards of self-satisfaction, no matter what you are paid, is the true measure of the work you do, whether in love, your career, or your life.

Love in a Less-Than-Perfect World

Top speaker Layne Longfellow claims that reality does not live up to expectations. As Oscar Wilde said, "The bride's second disappointment is Niagara Falls." Long-time top sales trainer Alan Cimberg says he hears much the same complaints from the different companies he has worked with in the last few years, whether they are making computers or selling building supplies:

☆ Our territories are too large (or too small).

☆ We need more help; we don't get enough support.

No company is perfect. As long as you're accepting a paycheck, you should keep your gripes to yourself and concentrate on some of the positive things about your company.

Bobbie Gee, corporate image consultant from Southern California, was flying home from Chicago and everything went wrong. There were many delays, and the flight was three hours behind schedule. One of the cargo doors was frozen, and there was no food in first class. The man sitting next to her complained all the way to Southern California about how that airline could do absolutely nothing right. Who was he? A pilot for the same airline!

Rekindling the Spark

It's very important to be centered in reality, in love or in a job. In any relationship, you have to work to feel the excitement on a continuing basis. You *need* excitement in your life. What did you do to keep the thrill in your love relationship? Perhaps the two of you relived your first date at that little country restaurant. Perhaps you thanked your loved one for just being there for you. Whatever you did, you got in touch with the person you first fell in love with.

The same kind of techniques applied to your career can rekindle the excitement you felt when you began your job. You must have had good reasons for taking the job in the first place. What were they? Make a list of them and start experiencing those things again in your daily routine.

In Japan, workers gather each morning to cheer their company before they go to their workstations. It's hard to imagine rows of corporate American employees doing the same thing, but you can lead your own personal cheering section. Begin each day expecting to have a productive, exciting day. Wasn't that how you used to arrive at your job in the morning? If you really expect to be productive during the day, very little will keep you from it.

There are many ways that we can keep both relationships and jobs exciting, challenging—and still be realistic. (Ultimately, of course, your happiness depends on how good you feel about yourself in the context of your job, a relationship, or just plain living.) It's too easy to get trapped by immediate goals. Stay aware of what is out there on the horizon, and adjust your actions when plans don't seem to be working according to your expectations.

Squandered Talent

"Lilies that fester," William Shakespeare said, "smell far worse than weeds." When the sweetest things on earth "turn sourest by their deeds," there is no bigger waste or greater shame. Squandered talent is a terrible thing. In a letter to his daughter, F. Scott Fitzgerald wrote: "All I believe in in life is the rewards for virtues (according to your talents), and the punishments for not fulfilling your duties, which are doubly costly."

There are indeed rewards for virtue just as there are costly punishments for shirking our duties. I see virtue in the effort of each of us to find ourselves, to make ourselves useful, to set our goals, to go about our work and our lives. Duty doesn't mean a loss of freedom, because duty requires self-discipline, and self-discipline is the key to personal freedom.

The Mystical Click

Making ourselves available to opportunities represents a major breakthrough in our adult life. A child will look at the funny symbols under the pictures in books and suddenly realize that they have meaning. Similarly, we can hear over and over about how we control our own lives and never really believe it, until — suddenly — something clicks. All the axioms, clichés, and vaguely perceived ideas suddenly shift and come into sharp focus, creating a vivid, three-dimensional picture of who we are and where we are going. When we make ourselves available to opportunity, we put ourselves that much closer to this realization. It is this "click," this near-mystical moment, that changes us forever.

Patricia Fripp, CPAE.

At your sales meeting or convention, Patricia talks about common sense that is often not such common practice. No complicated theories — just real life examples entertainingly presented in a free-wheeling style.

The Woman: She's the modern version of Horatio Alger — success out of obscurity. Twenty-year-old Fripp arrived in the U.S. with nothing more than tons of talent and spunk, a British accent and $500. Today she's a successful entrepreneur, author, speaker, and active participant in the San Francisco business community.

CPAE: The highest award given for professionalism and excellence in speaking, given by the National Speakers Association.

Topics for your meeting or convention:
- ☆ Adapting to Change
- ☆ Creative Thinking for Better Business
- ☆ Take Charge of Your Future

Style: High-energy, dynamic, witty and versatile.

Audience: Comfortable with groups from 10 to 3,000. Keynotes, half-day, full-day formats.

For further information, call us at:

(800) 634-3035 (Nationwide)
(800) 553-6556 (in California) or (415) 753-6556.

Or write to:

National Coordinator, Take Charge of Your Life, Inc.,
527 Hugo Street, San Francisco, CA 94122.

Or to listen to Patricia:

- ☆ 6-pack: 'Creative Thinking for Better Business,' $75.00
- ☆ 6-pack: 'Patricia Fripp on Speaking,' $75.00
- ☆ 6-pack: 'Express Yourself with Flair,' $75.00